GRIGORI GRABOVOI

NUMBER SERIES FOR PSYCHOLOGICAL NORMALIZATION
Book 1

The work «Number series for psychological normalization» was created by Grigori Petrovich Grabovoi in Russian in 2003. Was complemented by Grabovoi G.P.

Translation from Russian into English was made by PERMANENT CREATION

2013

Grigori P. Grabovoi
Number series for psychological normalization. Book1 – 2012, 208p

All rights reserved.
No part of the book may be reproduced in any form without the prior written consent of copyright owner.

ISBN-13: 978-1490431598
ISBN-10: 1490431594

GRIGORI GRABOVOI®
© Grabovoi G.P., 2004
© Grabovoi G.P., English translation, 2013

Introduction

The work contains sections on psychodiagnostics, psychotherapy, social psychology, psychology of labor, pathopsychology, psychophysics, defectology, perceptual psychology, personality psychology, psychoanalysis, motivational psychology, psychology of memory, psychology of emotions, feelings and thoughts, psychology of perception and sensations.

The methods of regulation of events in the process of an eternal development of man are given in the work by means of numerical rows correlated to the terms and notions, which are used in terms of psychology.

In case when the term denotes with some deviation from the standard (norm), then by means of a numerical row corresponding to the term, the norm that organizes the eternal development in generally accepted constructive direction is achieved. If the term denotes the description of the process, the numerical rows then can be taken for the usage of this description in the direction of eternal development. The described process by means of the numerical row may be applied for the providing of eternal development.

The psychology of eternal development differs by the fact that through the methods of psychology the main laws of eternal development materializes, the laws which comprise immortality of all live, resurrection and provide it in the sphere of life's work of a person. This psychological aspect, for which the form of finite relations is changed into eternal to direct psychology to the organization of this transition and its functioning when the laws of eternal development are carried out.

Psychology of eternal development forms social ties of society and laws, which provide the real eternal development of a man and mankind.

The ways (methods) of regulation in the direction of eternal development are following:

© Grabovoi G.P., 2003

1. Numerical rows which located after the term or notion, you can read, pronounce mentally or hum mentally in such a way that the sound of tune you perceive in some distance from your physical body. The melody may be any you like or you can just know that the tune is produced but you don't perceive some certain melody. The sphere of your thinking may have various forms of spheroid structures.

It is desirable to perceive the form of your running (controlling) thought that correlates to the term, somewhere near your body, and move or modify this form to get a result.

The methods of eternal development allow to receive the events of eternal development achievement already in the course of cognition of technologies of eternal development. Carrying out actions with such forms you must understand that they can be used for improvement of health and rescue (salvation) if you imagine near them yourself or a person who need to be healthier or be rescued. When you imagine yourself among these forms, you make yourself younger. The more control forms you can take into your consciousness in the course of psychological regulation numerical rows usage the faster your rejuvenation goes.

When you imagine that thought-forms of eternal development touch the other person you rejuvenate this person. The transfer from self-perception to the perception of another person in the psychology of eternal development can take some period of time, rich of knowledge of great value of information, because in the eternal development the constant increasing of information amount about surrounding goes. So it is important to perceive information without any tension, just fix your thought of it.

You can interpret a number as a thought; at that realizing the numerical row balances the time of your action for perception of reality by your comprehension with any volume of information. Such training for taking a number from a thought allows you to transfer events to a form accepted from the point of view of eternal development. When your attention is concentrated, you can see what events may be compressed in a number. So you can realize that it is impossible to compress an image of a man in a number, the number does not correspond to the person.

Such development of your perception can lead to the thought that the person is out of any reality of finite features, that is, the man is eternal. At this moment you must clearly imagine the numerical row 888, then 898, then the number 1, the next number 2 and at the number 3 you must understand that there is the sphere of information through which you can make reality eternal by means of the number. This reality starts from a man and vice versa, the eternity of environment helps the man to realize his eternity.

Such understanding helps to realize that in rehabilitation of the person with numerical rows the person changes the World by his will in the direction of eternal development, opening his primordial eternal essence, the essence is able to create the eternal immortal body. So, through the knowledge received with the help of the number, you come to the spiritual inner state that means your eternity. Then from such inner state the person can get the same ones also in cases when you do not use the number.

Logically, from the quantity of numbers, you perceive the sign of endlessness which is separated from the certain number. Symbolic form defined in the terms of psychology of regulation through the use of numbers allows you to recognize the variants of future events which lead to eternity in any case. The phase of controlling prognosis when using the numerical rows of psychological normalization must coincide with the information of the event just fulfilled in future, all elements of which are eternal.

Forms of thoughts can be modified very fast or instantaneously in the technologies of eternal development. That is you can perceive already modified form and the primary form you perceive later. The principle of construction of physical matter of a man towards eternal development is also based on the fact that the events of the matter future time are comprehended faster than the events of the past.

The psychological base of this principle consists in the fact that for the realization of the inner, coming from the soul task of endless development one must be able to manage physical matter in future. And the period of time for making the solving may be limited. But in the same time, for the information of the past one can create the direction of special acts using the needed time. With regard to events of the future it is expediently to accomplish a regulative control in advance and if it is necessary to correct the situation in real time.

The creator of the action is united with temporal periods in the event of achieved aim. You may the same way by means of numerical rows of psychological regulation memorize some inner (spiritual) state corresponding to the achieved result. One can use such inner state according to the term or generalize it for normalization and focus of events on the sphere of endless development.

One can read the whole book for the over-all comprehension that reinforced the control of eternal life. The knowledge of terminology in the area of psychology allows you to estimate a lot from the point of view of accepted notions which simplifies the achievement of objective forms of eternal development and widens the sphere used for controlling understanding, when there is a need to try to understand everything that occurs in such way so as to reach the actuality which proves your ability to use the methods of eternal development.

2. If there are gaps in the row of numbers it is possible for the achievement of the result of one aim to use the whole row at first, and then the parts of the row divided with the gap. You can make little pauses in the places of gaps when you utter mentally the numbers of the row. If there are no gaps in the row one can imagine the gap between every three numbers and make the same actions as with the rows with gaps.

3. Put the numbers of the row above the numbers of

current date and concentrate on two rows at once.

4. Comparing the numerical rows that correspond to the different terms and notions you can define (in place where numbers are correlated) the interrelation and the possibility of their mutual correlation in the way of eternal development among different objects and events, described in these terms and notions.

5. You can imagine the numbers of the row in such a way that, for example, apples put in your hands from the number and different apples of the same sort correspond to different numbers and their combinations. Then one need to make an effort and perceive through numbers that there is an objective reality including the concrete images under you control of eternal development.

6. The process of rejuvenation can be carried out in the following way:

6.1. Imagine that numbers corresponding to one term are placed from the shoulder to the hand of the right arm.

6.2. Imagine that numbers corresponding to the term that follows the term described in clause 6.1 are on the skin of the left arm.

6.3. Feel how the light from numbers of the left hand passes to the numbers of the right hand. In the moment of movement of this light through the zone of chest try to understand how you solve the psychological context of eternal development for yourself and for others.

7. The technologies of resurrection are progressed to the obligatory realization by means of quick combination and altering of numerical rows, corresponding to different terms and notions, in your memory and visual perception. The main in this action is to keep in mind the main aim and not to divert from it while quick reading of numerical rows. In due course you can reach such level of perfection, when the concentration on the aim in your memory turns it to the reality.

8. The principles and practice of ever-living are realized in the following way:

8.1. The principle of ever-living is considered taken in the conjunction with the practice and is following the logics of happened events. Because your perception always keeps the information about some event, you can consider that the principle of eternity is in the event, and the practice is in your further thinking. Linking the past event by means of numerical row with possible or psychologically desired future you get the psychological state of presence in conscious eternity. You transfer this psychological state to all endless future. When you learn to do it quite easy, you will get the state which controls the eternal development. This state produces the quality of spirit, which you can interpret as spiritual self-learning of eternal life in usual everyday life.

8.2. For ever-living you can imagine in front of every row you use 888, 9 and numbers 1 and 9 written in words.

9. You can make the improving of the health just adding numbers 319 and the numbers of a current date (in order: year, month, date) after the row of psychological normalization you use.

A

Abasia 814817 914212 31 – disturbance of the ability to walk with elements of walking movement skills retained.

Absence (absentia) 518916 319717 81 – short-term fatigue, blocking of consciousness.

Abstinence 528419 319718 23 – state arising from the termination of alcohol or drugs effect when there is a sadden break of their admitting.

Sexual abstinence 298714 318922 51– the state of the subject deprived of an opportunity to lead a sex life.

Abstraction 819314 919814 312 – the cognitive process as one of the main operations of thinking; it consists in allocation of certain features of the studied holistic object and distraction from all the rest.

Abulia 419316 019817 311 – pathological disturbance of mental regulation of psychic actions, psychopathological syndrome expressed as lethargy, disorder of volitional impulse, absence of desires and stimulus of activities, inability to make a decision and produce proper action although the need for it is realized.

Avokaliya 518 514 318912 512 – form of motor amusia at which one lost the ability to perform melodies with voice or musical instruments.

Autoagression 5148 714 318 912 81 – type of aggressive behavior and aggressive actions of the subject aimed at himself. It is manifested by self- accusation, self-abasement, causing body self harm and suicidal behavior.

Autohypnosis 512 319 419817 47 – (self-hypnosis) Self-hypnosis is the hypnosis caused by autosuggestion on the contrary to the hetherohypnosis caused by actions of another person.

Autocratism 514 317 814918 9 – the social and psychological characteristic of the individual reflecting an authority, power, propensity to use undemocratic methods of influence on people in forms of orders, instructions, penalties and so on.

Automation 498714 319814 914 – transition of executed action at the level of unconscious control when the main role goes to the perceptions and sensations, especially kinesthetic ones.

Automatism 589318 714917 31 – (unconscious automatism) the actions to be implemented without the direct participation of consciousness, happened 'of themselves' out of conscious control.

Authoritarianism 514901609 – social and psychological characteristics of individual reflecting its aspiration to the utmost subject to influence of partners of interaction and communication.

Authoritarian 518 396 749810 – Individual characteristics of subject or his behavior towards other people which distinguishes the tendency to assert his power and authority.

Authority 59481737 – 1.Influence, power of an individual based on the occupied position, status etc. In terms of social psychology in this regard the concept is often correlated with notion of power. 2. Acceptance of the individual right to make decision under conditions of common activity. In this sense the concept may not coincide with authority: a person may have the authority even if he is not endowed with appropriate powers whether he serves as a kind of moral standard and therefore has a high degree of reference for other people.

Authoritativeness 914 881712 – Ability to be of certain importance among other people and to be for them the source of ideas and enjoy their respect and recognition.

Autoscopy 594 899 706541 – parapsychological term means the appearing of individual feeling as if he sees himself from outside. This phenomenon occurs when sensing of excessive fatigue even whether a person has no mental deviations.

Autosuggestion 519 311 – suggestion exercised by a person for himself (self-suggestion). It supposes the combination of a suggestor and subject of suggestion in one person.

Autotraining 498 017 999067 – autogenic training.

Autoerotism 538744898712 – term meaning the first phase of child sex life for which he uses various methods of sexual satisfaction with parts of his own body when external object is completely absent.

Agglutination 519048 71042819 – one of the essential characteristics of words used for inner speech. One of the ways to create imaginative visions. Any qualities, characteristics, parts, features are combined in one image. As the result there can be very fancy image at times far from reality.

Aggravation 316718916888 – exaggeration by the individual of severity of symptoms of the real disease or sickness of his state.

Agent 599047889310 – when extrasensory practicing the subject who must address something to percipient.

Agnosia 599806719 319 - the state when the brain cannot decode the information received from normally functioning receptors.

Visual agnosia 488901 317 489 – neuropathological disorder. The typical is loss of ability to perceive visual items (or their pictures) and events of reality, although visual acuity is still sufficiently retained.

Acoustic agnosia 589477918371 neuropsychological violation, typical for which is loss of ability to identify sounds, phonemes and noises.

Social agnosia 598428317489 – personal attitude to his own life when he does not perceive positive sides of life and is not able to organize his activity so that it brings him satisfaction.

Tactile agnosia 5994780798 – neuropsychological disorder, the typical for which is loss of ability to adequate percept of objects to the touch with sufficient adequacy of some individual tactile sensations, sense of form, mass, temperature.

Agoraphobia 909841319 8049 - a kind of neurosis

characterized by pathological fear of open spaces, squares etc.

Agrammatism 9014089184778 – neuropsychological disorder, typical for which is loss of ability of speech grammatical structure analysis and grammatically correct use of speech.

Agrafia 317488918710 – violation of writing appearing in various disorders of speech. It is manifested either as full loss of ability to write or a rude distortion of words, missing of syllables and letters, as an inability to put the letters and syllables in words etc.

Aggressiveness 519061 718910 - one of the congenital attitudes rooted in sadistic phase of libido. It is expressed as the effort of offensive or violent actions, aimed at inflicting a damage or destruction of an object of attack.

Aggression 528471 228911 – individual or collective behavior or the action directed to inflicting of physical or psychological harm or even to the destruction of a person or a group.

Verbal aggression 978316918 71 – the form of aggressive behavior when one uses the expression of his negative emotions by means of appropriate intonation and the nonverbal components of speech as well as threatening content of speech.

Instrumental aggression 598777 888999016 – aggressive behavior when aggressive actions are not the expression of emotional condition: the aim of the action of a subject who expresses his aggression is neutral and aggression applies only as a way to achieve the goal.

Indirect aggression 513718 91388901 – aggressive behavior the targeting of which against a person is hidden or is not recognized by the subject of aggression.

Direct aggression 00598714 318 914 – the behavior of violent intentional nature the purpose of which is not hidden.

Reactive aggression 489713519616 - arises as a subject's reaction to frustration. It is accompanied by emotional states of anger, hostility hatred etc.

Physical aggression 598755898055 – aggressive behavior when physical power is used against another person or object.

Adaptation 519487917917 - 1. Adaptation of structure and functions of an organism, its organs and cells to the conditions of environment, aimed at preservation of homeostasis. 2. Adaptation of sensory organs to the peculiarities of influencing stimuli for their optimal perception and protection of receptors from overload.

Psychological adaptation 591478918988912 – adaptation of a person to the demands and criteria of values existing in society at the expense of the appropriation of standards and values of the given society.

Sensory adaptation 498016 714213 – the change of sensitivity of analyzer served for its tuning up to the intensity of stimulus; in general, adaptive change of sensitivity for the intensity of irritant. It is manifested in various subjective effects. It can be achieved at the expense of increasing or reduction of common sensitivity. It is characterized by the range of alteration of sensitivity, the speed of this alteration and selectivity of changes according to the adaptive impact. Physiologic changes which are on the base of adaptation touch either peripheral or central links of analyzer. The combination of neuropsychological and psychophysical methods has a great value for the investigation of the mechanism of sensual adaptation and the processes of perception in general.

Social integration 548321819911 – constant process of person's integration in society, the process of active adaptation of the individual toward social conditions and also the result of this process. The correlation of these components which defines the manners and behavior depends on aims and valuable positioning of the individual and on possibilities of their achievement in social environment. As a result the formation of self-consciousness and role-behavior, the ability of self-control and self-service, the ability of adequate communication with others are reached.

Adaptiveness 319016 819728 – tendencies of operation of purposeful system defined by correlation or non-correlation of its aims and results achieved in the course of activity. Adaptivity is expressed as their coordination.

Social and cultural adaptiveness 891488319 712 – when using for tests it means correspondence of test's tasks and test's marks, received according to them, to the peculiarities of cultures, formed in society where the test is used. It includes either the change of test's tasks themselves or the amplification of test's norms. This requirement is important when borrowing of the test from another country.

Additivity 591 668 889 319 – feature of values, consisting in the characteristic or the value corresponding to the whole object is always equal to the sum of values corresponding to its parts however the object may be divided into parts.

Adrenalin(e) 591 814 848 321 – hormone produced by the cerebral substance of suprarenal glands. Its stimulating impact on the organism is compared with the action of sympathetic nervous system.

Agitation 291 814 888917 312 – affective reaction arising in the answer to the threat for life, accidental situation and other psychogenic factors. It is manifested in the form of strong anxiety, uneasiness, loss of purposeful actions. A person fidgets and becomes to be able to do only simple automatic actions. The feeling of vacuum and absence of thoughts arises, the possibility of reasoning to establish sophisticated ties among phenomena is damaged. It is accompanied with real vegetative declinations; it appears paleness, quickened pulse, tremor of hands, fast breath etc.

Acalculia 284061 718 329 488 – neuropsychological symptom typical for which is violation of count and calculating operations as the result of damage of different areas of cerebral cortex.

Accommodation 298 388014712 – 1. Mechanism consisting in the change of existing scheme for its adaptation to new object or situation. In particular it is the change of curvature of crystalline lance for precise focus of a picture on retina. 2. Change of already established knowledge, skills according to new conditions.

Acceleration 598069 788 061 – the acceleration of somatic development and physiologic maturation of children and teenagers; expressed as increasing of mass and dimensions of body (also newborns), as accelerated puberty.

Act of apperception 188917319871 – the process of organization of the item of higher level: consciousness is able even infinitely to be full with some content if it actively unites into more and more large items. The ability for enlargement of items is found not only for simplest perceptual processes but also for thinking.

Ideomotor action 918714319848 – the transfer of an image of muscles movement into real producing of this movement, in other words, arising of nervous impulses, providing the movement as soon as the image of it appears. These facts are involuntary, unconscious and usually have slightly expressed space features.

Activation 594887319827 – state of nervous system which characterizes the degree of its stimulation and reactivity. It is defined by modulating effects coming from the part of nervous system which encloses the limbic system and the structures of cerebral reticular system. Together with balance of these impacts changes the intensiveness and the qualitative peculiarity of activation fixed on vegetative indices, such as arterial tension, frequency of pulse, skin resistance, breath changes etc are altered.

Activation: individual level – 891488918917 – usual for every person level of activation on the background of which the activity is mainly realized. This level is the natural determinant of individuality.

Activation: optimal level – 591788 319488 – level of maximum correspondence of nervous system state to the behavior act as the result of which the high effectiveness of its performance is achieved.

© Grabovoi G.P., 2003

Psychological activation 81972888998217 – prolongation of the psychological activation. It is connected with decoding of external signals depending on awakening level and on consciousness state as well as needs, preferences, interest and targeting.

Physiological activation 598789988481 - It is connected to the function of centers, presented in the base of cortex. The mechanisms of awakening are connected with these centers; it is at the level where the signals coming from outer world and from the organism are selected and classified before their sending to the cerebral cortex whether they are quite important. Activation of the highest centers gives the organism property to keep awake and to keep up with the signals from external world what provides it with the preservation of physiologic and psychic balance.

Capability 519788919489 – characteristic of nervous system which is defined by unconditional-reflex balance of the processes of nervous stimulation and inhibition and which is tightly associated with the level of nonspecific activation of cortex. It is interpreted as integral feature of nervous system.

Activity 589398719888 - the notion expresses the ability of living creatures to produce voluntary motions which is to be changed under the influence of external and internal stimuli-irritants – common feature of living creatures, their own dynamics as the source of transformation or support of life-essential ties with environment. In terms of psychology it exists in accordance with activity, being found as dynamic condition of its formation, implementation and modification as the feature of its own movement.

Super situational activity 298481718 318 - ability to rise above the level of requirements of situation, to put aims. Inner and external limitations are overriding through the use of it. It is seen as phenomena of creative work, cognitive activity, selfless risk, above permitted standard activity.

General activity 84197918712814 – one of the areas of manifestation of temperament. It is defined by the intensiveness and value of interaction of a person with physical and social environment. As to this parameter one can be inert, passive, calm, initiative, active, striving etc.

Detached activity 598881488012 – certain neutralization of a human being's activity, when he experiences the inner or outer impact on him and the separation of the person from the results of his activity occurs. For instance it is posthypnotic behavior.

Searching activity 566890789 128 – behavior aimed at the alternation of the situation or relation to it in the absence of certain prognosis of its result, but when constant controlling of its effectiveness. There are all variety of active-defense behavior, self-stimulation and orientative behavior for animals. Psychic manifestation of researching activities is the important part of the process of planning, fancy etc in regard to a human society.

Mental activity: biorhythm 319817919227 – (biorhythms of human psychic activity) – periodic alternation of the person's psychic activity state of tension and relaxation.

Abnormal activity 2489067180 1987 – one of the form of manifestation of over state activity. It is expressed as striving of the person or the group to raise the claims laid by the society to some kind of activity. Abnormal activity is one of the most important indexes of high effectiveness of the group; it characterizes the group as the real group.

Actualization 498712 888 189 – the action consisting in the extraction of adopted material from the short or longtime memory for its next use for recognition, remembering or its instant reproduction. It is characterized by different degree of difficulty or easiness which depends on the level of keeping or forgetting of the extracted content.

To actualize 591 488 611 098 71 – to transfer from potential state to the real actual state.

Historic actuality 591 398 719 411 – individual ability to utmost cooperation in the course of social-cultural processes with minimum damage of own individuality and activity of its defensive mechanisms. It overtakes and excludes primitive notions about some mutual necessity to make a sacrifice of people in the name of social progress.

Psychological acoustics 591 489319718 – part of the experimental psychology dedicated to the investigation of sensations in response to acoustic stimuli.

Physiological acoustics 519 317 819 481 – part of the physiology of sensory organs. It is dedicated to the investigation of regularities of the sound perception and construction of speech.

Emphasis 519 317 918 – one of the methods of creation of pictures of imagination. A detail or part of the whole separated and becoming dominative, bearing the main meaning. Example is caricatures etc.

Accentuation 598421 – isolation, underlining of some feature or attribute on the background of others, its special development. In terms of psychology it is a little exaggerated but in frames of psychological norm, development of some psychological features or peculiarities of the subject.

Asthenic accentuation 5980912 488 916 - characteristic quick weariness, irritation, inclination to depression and hypochondria.

Hypertemic accentuation 599048 –continuously elevated mood, high psychic activity with striving for activity and tendency to dissipate one's energies, not to finish the work entirely are typical for it.

Dysthemic accentuation 918749318612 – predominance of low mood, inclination to depression, concentration on mournful and dismal sides of life are typical for it.

Hysteroid accentuation 498748916318 (histrionic accentuation) –expressed tendency to repression of facts and events unpleasant for the individual, to lying, pretence, fantasy generation used to attract somebody's attention, tendency to adventurism, vanity, escape in illness in case of unsatisfied need of recognition are typical for it.

Compulsive accentuation 89131488 99 00 1 – excessive subordination and dependence on opinions of another people, avolition and lack of criticism, inclination to conservatism are typical for it.

Labile accentuation 489 216 –sharp change of mood in dependence on situation is typical for it.

Accentuation unstable 459 5178 – characterized by inclination to yield to influence of another people, constant search for new impressions, groups, the habit to establish contacts of superficial character easily.

Paranoid accentuation 319 008 6197 – characterized by high suspiciousness and painful resentfulness, stability of negative effects, drive to dominate, hostility to another opinions; and as a result high proneness to conflict.

Psychasthenic accentuation 5948917214 – typical are high uneasiness, weakness, suspiciousness, inclination to self analysis, to constant reasoning and doubtfulness, tendency to formation of obsessions and ritual acts.

Sensitive accentuation 598412688914 – characterized by high impressionability, timidity (fear), harsh feeling of self-inferiority.

Accentuation cycloid 918016718717 – characterized by alternation of phases of good and bad mood with different period.

Accentuation schizoid 519 311899216 – characterized by separatism, estrangement, introversion, emotional coolness expressing in difficulties in establishing of emotional contacts; lack of intuition in the process of communication.

Accentuation epileptic 219317919817 - characterized by inclination to spiteful-depressing mood with increasing aggression expressing as attacks of anger and rage (sometimes with elements of brutality); proneness to conflicts, sticky thinking, pedantry.

Acceptor of action 594817994317 8 – hypothetic psychophysiologic apparatus i.e. psychological mechanism of foreseeing and estimation of the results of actions in functional systems. It causes the organization of motor activity of an organism in behavior act and displays the model of future result of the action that is 'informational equivalent of the result'.

Alalia — 519319 018716314 — neuropsychological symptom characterizing by absence or lack of development of children speech which are able to hear normally and are of sufficient level of intellect. Alalia is conditioned by damages of the speech zones of cerebral cortex during the birth, illnesses or cerebral traumas during prevocalic period of life.

Algorithm 514312 - prescription giving on the base of the system of rules, the consequence of operations, the precise fulfillment of which allows solving tasks of certain class. In terms of psychology when learning of processes of management and procedures of fulfillment of prescriptions for various types of activity. Includes the notion to initial data that are necessary for solving the task, or to the rule according to which the process of finding the result is considered to be finished. The ability to complete the task in general i.e. mastery of some general techniques of making the tasks of certain class means the mastery of some algorithm.

Alexithymia 519318 814 317 - inability of a subject to name emotions experienced by himself or others, that is to transfer them into verbal aspect.

Alexia 299481319711 - violation of reading, confusion of ability to read — inability to read a text in spite of literacy; or inability to obtain the process of reading. Appears as damages of different sections of cortex of the left hemisphere (for right-handed)

Alcoholism 148543292 - abuse of alcohol.

Alcoholism and drug addiction: psychological prevention 148543292 5194 5194 — psychological methods of prophylaxis of alcoholism and drug addiction.

Alcoholism symptomatic 148543292 228 – development of alcoholism on the background of another psychic illness — for example, schizophrenia.

Alcoholism chronic 148543292317 914 — In chronic

alcoholism according to the measure of addiction to alcohol, the manifestations of abstinence are increased, psychic and physiological dependence on the doses of alcohol are appeared (strong need in alcohol with the aim to escape phenomena of psychic and physical discomfort appearing in abstinence from alcohol), step by step there pathologic changes in inner organs appear, disorders of metabolism, damages of peripheral nerves, functional organic changes in central nervous system. Social and psychic degradation increases, alcoholic epilepsies and alcoholic psychosis are appeared.

Alcoholic antonymic 489411319811 – social organization, uniting alcohol addicters who express their readiness to be cured from alcoholism by themselves and help others and their relatives in it.

Albinism 519317 819 887421 - inheritable anomaly of a person or animals, characterized by partial or complete absence of skin pigmentation, irises and hair, fair and wool. Caused by absence of tyrosine participating in synthesis of melanin.

Altruism 498717319887 - system of human orientation of values in which the central motive and criteria of moral judgment – are the interests of other person or social group. The central idea of altruism is the idea of unselfishness as ungrammatical oriented activity, carrying out in the interests of other people and not supposing real compensation.

Alpha-rhythm 519 314 – the rhythm of encephalogram in the state of approximate calm. It has frequency 8-13 Hz and average amplitude 30-70 μV- with periodic increasing and decreasing. It is stimulated by thalamic cerebral and intra cerebral processes. The analysis of alpha-rhythm characteristics is important in research of cognitive processes, age dynamics and individual peculiarities.

Alfa-training 498799009611 – psychotherapeutic technique, based on the inverse biological. It consists in teaching according to the schedule of instrumental conditioning of regulation of such psychophysiologic processes that considered to be inaccessible to conscious control before.

Ambivalence 319814819311 – (ambiguity) – duality, double meaning, sometimes contradiction. In terms of psychology means dual experience, attached presence in the spirit of two contradicting, as if incompatible intentions to one object – for example, sympathy and antipathy.

Ambivalence emotional 591489 718 14 – non-coordination, contradictoriness of some simultaneously experienced senses to some object; contradicting attitude of the subject to object – simultaneous orientation of contradicting sensations at one and the same object. The complex of emotional states associated with duality of relations – with simultaneous acceptance and rejection.

Ambidexterity 391814919007 – inborn or trained leveled development of the function of both hands – without emphasis of the leading hand.

Ambition – disorder of consciousness activity 4180981917 8 – state of its incoherence characterized by: 1) full loss of orientation in external world when a person lost self-consciousness and remembering of new information is damaged; 2) motor exaggeration; 3) hallucinations; 4) absence of memories about this state, when it passes away.

Amimia 419317819917 – reduction or inhibition of mimic, appearing in illnesses of nervous system and some psychic diseases. Amimia, appearing in damage of extra pyramid system is the manifestation of violation of motor components of emotional reactions and is a part of the syndrome of general akinesia. When frontal lobes of cortex damaged it is aroused by violation of emotional sphere and is a part of lobe syndrome.

Amnesia 41854328 – memory disorders expressed as partial loss of ability to preserve in memory new coming information. Embrace periods from some minutes to some years. Show as various local cerebral disorders.

Amnesia anterograde 418543298 – memory

disorder for events which were taking place after the beginning of the disease or after trauma. The brain lost the ability to transfer information from short-time to long-time memory. It can enclose various periods of time.

Amnesia defensive 4185432319 – memory disorders expressed as ousting of unpleasant, traumatic former experience.

Amnesia infantile 418543252 1 – specific form of amnesia; in most of people it embraces the first years of childhood through 6-8th year of life.

Amnesia hysterical 4984185432 – specific form of amnesia in neurotic, the source of which – is the infantile amnesia.

Amnesia posthypnotic 41854321 – memory disorders, expresses forgetting of events, taken place in time of hypnosis diagnostic treatment interview.

Amnesia retrograde 4185432418 – expressed as memory disorders for events, preceding to disease or trauma; the events which were taking place during some hours, days and sometimes years before the disease, are forgotten.

Amnesia experimental 94185432 – the method to check various hypothesis of memory functioning, where pharmacological means, hypoxia, electroshock are used as amnesic. At the expense of their action the electric activity, providing the preservation of a trace in short-time memory is interrupted, and its transfer to long-time memory is prevented.

Amok 9184819 – ethno specific term, meaning psychopathological syndrome, characterized by sudden appearance of panic with change of consciousness (as a type of twilight consciousness) and uncontrolled strive to move in one direction, damaging and destroying everything on his way, and killing those who prevents it. It continues while the patient will be stopped or while he fall from fatigue.

Amusia 498017 – loss of ability to understand and play music, to read and write music letters. Appears as damage of temporal parts of cerebral right hemisphere (for right-hand) caused by violations of music hearing. Expressed as irrecognition of known melodies, in difficulty of perception and reproduction of rhythmic sound combinations. Often combined with acoustic agnosia as a result of which usual sounds and noises stop to be differed.

Anaclisis 498317814218 – notion means excessive emotional dependence of an individual on other people. He experiences that his thoughts, senses and drives appear simultaneously with appearance of the same states in people with whom he is in analytic tie. This phenomenon is interpreted as the regression of behavior to the degree of child unity with mother when such tie was natural.

Analysis 3198 – process of fragmentation of the whole object or phenomenon into constituent parts – in aspect of thought images or material modeling. Analysis is tightly associated with synthesis.

Active analysis 31978 – method of psychotherapy incorporates elements of psychoanalysis (first of all the associative method) and other psychotherapeutic techniques.

Analysis bioenergetics 898317418 – the form of body-oriented psychotherapy. While analysis is carried out, at first, there one put the task to define the type of character that is to find in corporal organization of a client the parts, where in case of muscles tensions there is no normal movement of "psychic" energy. After this the work comes to the construction of a new body at the expense of the exercises based on tension and relaxation of certain muscles, breath release; somatic expression of emotions. It is supposed that psychic energy associated with before with muscles tension can come again into disposition of the client.

Analysis graphological 598421918411 – reveal of individual-psychological variability of handwriting. It is used for identification of scripts (signatures) and for to define psychic states or characterological peculiarities of the author of manuscript.

Analysis variance 419 4118 – in terms of psychology – the statistic method allowing to analyze the influence of various factors on dependent variable. The essence of variance analysis consists in dispersion of measured character into independent parts each of which characterizes the impact of some factor or their interaction. The following comparison of such parts allows to estimate the meaningfulness of each factor and their combinations.

Analysis categorical 214217814318 – in terms of psychology – the method of study of the development of psychological cognition as activity, the elements of which are concrete-scientific categories, reproducing various sides of psychic reality: image, action, motive etc.

Analysis causal-dynamic 918317418978 – methodology strategy – devoted for extraction of the unity of psychic: differs from usual analysis, which disintegrates the whole into separate elements and the quality of wholeness is lost, in causal-dynamic analysis the such minimal element is considered, in which the whole is still existed.

Analysis qualitative 419718918912 – the method of psychological investigations, not using quantitative results but making conclusions only on the base of logical reasoning about the received facts.

Analysis cluster 498 311 819217 – mathematic procedure of multi-measure analysis, allowing on the base of quantity of results, characterizing the set of objects, blocking them to clusters so that objects inside the class will be more homogenous than objects of different classes. On the base of numerical parameters of objects the distances among them, expressed as Euclid metrics or in others are counted. The method is widely used in psycholinguistic.

Analysis control 91891791987 – psychoanalytic procedure, serving the aims of professional training of psychoanalysts, in which future psychoanalyst participates as a probationer on the second year of study. And he himself carries out psychoanalytic sessions with a client, but after each session he discusses it with his teacher, and for this he uses stenographic notes, where the dialog with the client and probationer's comments are fixed.

© Grabovoi G.P., 2003

Analysis short 519515819891 – the form of psychoanalysis, characterized by orientation to only local themes, the actuality of which was defined on the stage of preliminary psychodiagnostic. The main procedures of its fulfillment are analysis of free associations and the transfer. The application of the short analysis is especially effective in quite light forms of neurotic symptoms and in actual psychological conflicts.

Analysis correlation 319317819817 – the statistic method of estimation of form, sign and how much is the tie of examined features or factors. It allows for the very short time to receive a quantity of results for sufficient number of tested persons. It is applied in some special cases, when experimental way is difficult or even impossible – for example, due to moral reasons. It allows to get information, based on more various extractions and closer to the existing in society reality – in difference from laboratory experiments.

Analysis of peculiarities of speech communication 491874319887 – one of the projective techniques belongs to the group of methods of researching of expression.

Analysis of handwriting 4193179198 – one of the projective techniques belongs to the group of methods study of expression.

Analysis direct 914 318901008 – the method of psychotherapy. The form of psychoanalysis specially oriented to the healing of schizophrenia. The typical feature of the method is striving to interpret psychoanalytically not only the client's dreams but all his actions: behavior, thoughts suddenly coming in his mind; various oddities and fancies.

Analysis regression 5193179182279 – the statistic method, allowing of research the dependence of the meaning of the middle of some value on the variation of another value or some values (in this case the multi-regression analysis is used). Regression analysis is applied mainly in empiric researches in solving of the tasks associated with the estimation of some influences (the influence of intellectual talent on progress, motives – on behavior), in construction of psychological tests etc.

Analysis system 319814 918217 – the approach to the research of objects and phenomena, expressing in their consideration as the developing system – with ousting of the structure of the system and laws of transformation and development of the system in whole.

Analysis transactional 598411 818 711 – psychoanalytically oriented branch of psychology. The method of research and treatment of emotional disorders, directed to the correction of interrelations with other people and overcoming of difficulties.

Analysis tuitional 519 5173198 – psychoanalytic procedure, serving the aims of education of highly qualified psychoanalysts. The future psychoanalyst participates in consulting of his teacher as a client.

Analysis factor 531488 918 – the method of multidimensional mathematic statistic, applied in research of statistically bound features with the aim to distinct the certain numbers of hidden from direct observation factors. With the help of the factor analysis not only the connection of change of one variable with the change of another is established but the measure of this connection is defined and the main factors, laying in the base of the noted changes are revealed.

Analysis existential 319314819 008 – one of the branch of modern psychoanalysis aimed at the research of personality in its wholeness and uniqueness of its existence. Existential analysis comes from the philosophic thesis that the real individual in a person is revealed only when he is free from causal ties with the world, social environment. Human existence is interpreted in the context of 3 time modes – past, present and future; symptoms of neurotic disorder appear when one of these modes prevails and it causes the narrowing of personal inner world and limitation of the horizon of its existential seeing.

Analyzer 498 614 33019 – definition of the functional unity responsible to perception and analysis of sensor information of some modality. Analyzer is the part of refectory apparatus which also includes: executive mechanism; the constellation of command neurons, motoneurons and motorial unites; and special neurons i.e. modulators changing the degree of stimulation of other neurons.

Taste analyzer 890 319718471 – neurophysiologic system the work of which provides special analysis of chemical substances coming to the oral cavity.

Analyzer motor 234891718411 – neurophysiologic system at the expense of which the analysis and synthesis of signals, coming from organs of motion is carried out. It participates in support of constant tonus of body muscles and coordination of motions.

Analogy 498712 8901 – Similarity between objects in some sense. Use of analogy in cognition – is the base for advancing of suppositions, hypothesis. Tasks to establish the analogy are in the context of psychodiagnostic researches. Difficulties in finding of similarity between objects according to abstract feature can be the mark of not sufficiently developed thinking or of its disorders.

Analgesia 219014 8901 519 – Reduction or full elimination of pain sensitivity.

Ananke 891714 219 372 – Actual need, natural necessity.

Androgen 498 071 319807 – Male reproductive (sex) hormones mainly produced in testicles. The most active is testosterone; it plays the important role in development of male genital organs.

Androgyny 989014 319788 – Notion for the definition of people successfully combined in themselves either traditional male and traditional female psychological qualities. Androgyny is the important psychological characteristic of a person, determining the ability to change his behavior depending on a situation. It helps for the formation of stress stability, when approaching of successes in various spheres of life activity.

Anesthetic 59189171 481 – Substance utilizable for repression of sensitivity to pain.

Anima 591048 789371 – a feminine.

Animism 898 319781 489087 – World outlook beliefs for which practically all objects which in some extent correlate to human activity are considered to be animate.

Animism childish 219014 319811 – Children visualization according to which even inanimate objects are animate. It is especially typical for children of 5years age and it is lost in further social and cognitive development.

Animus 214318819715 – masculine archetype in the feminine spirit.

Anomy 598712 819 301 – Notion for explanation of deviating behavior: suicides, apathy, disillusion, etc. It expresses by itself the historically conditioned process of destruction of basic elements of culture, first of all in the context of moral norms when quite sharply changing of social ideals and morality.

Anti-localizationism 891041519719 091 – Neuropsychological branch for which it was accepted that the cortex is the one and undifferentiated unity, the work of which causes the functioning of all psychic processes with equal facility. It was considered that when damaging of any zone of cortex, the general reduction of psychic functions goes, and its degree depends on the volume of damaged part.

Anti-psychiatry 391489 011 989 – Psychological doctrine and ideological study aimed at the demythologization, reveal and radical reconstruction of modern psychiatry as the mass form of violation.

Anticipation 2193178 – Ability of the system to foresee in some ways the development of events, phenomena and results of actions. In terms of psychology 2 notional aspects of the notion are differed: 1) the ability to imagine the possible result of the action before its fulfillment, and also to imagine the way of the problem solving before it will be really solved (intuition); 2) the ability of an organism to prepare to the reaction on some event till it comes; this waiting usually expressed as certain posture or movement and provided by the mechanism of the acceptor of action.

Anthropogenesis 219214 8179101 – Process of human origin, origin and development of all types of Homo, observed in logical and psychic context.

Anthropology 248318719 417 – Biological science of origin and evolution of physical organization of a man and human races. Sometimes the term is considered widely as the complex of sciences about man.

Anthropomorphism 918417 489217 – Idea about the psychic features existence for the animals as well as of abilities inherent only to a man.

Anthrophobia 498716 019811 – kind of neurosis characterized by pathological fear of people and a crowd.

Aneroziya 888017 918 341 – Absence of sexual libido.

Non-aesthetic 514 317 988 277 – deprived of sensuality.

Apathy 938 781 411 8779801 – State, characterized by emotional passivity, indifference, simplicity of feelings, disregard to environment and reduction of stimuli and interests. It flows on the background of reduced physical and psychological activity. It is formed as the result of long time psychic disorder, sometimes appears as some organic damages of cortex. It may be observed at mental debility, and as the result of prolonged somatic disease.

Apnea 841900 191 891 – More or less prolonged breath suppression.

Apparatus vestibular 219 398 481 711 – part of the ear labyrinth, including semicircle canals and two cavities i.e. sacculos and utriculos which are responsible for the perception of position and motions of the head.

Motional apparatus 914 718 019 487 – physiological system at the expense of which motions are constructed and fulfilled. It consists of a skeleton, muscles, nervous centers and afferent and efferent conduction tracts.

Psychological equipment 914 318 7190973214598 –

devices, mechanisms, equipment used for registration and measuring of psychic processes, functions and states.

Apperception 981 0191 38923109 – feature of perception, existing at the level of consciousness and characterizing the personal level of perception. It reflects the dependence of perception on the former experience and sets of an individual and on general content of human psychic activity and his individual peculiarities.

Apraxia 419 891 39980319 - violation of voluntary directed motions and actions, impossibility to make purposeful motions when normal intellect, motor and sensor systems' functioning.

Artifact 5194 3918019 99801 – phenomenon or effect, brought in to the experiment by a researcher.

Artifact of Mental Health Clinics 594 7128918 019 – special behavior disorders appearing in patients of psychic clinics as the reaction to new stress-producing situation which they make it into: coercion hospitalization, absence of conscious occupations, limitation of social contacts and etc.

Archetype 541 318 016 – the term of analytic psychology denoted the essence, form and the method of contact of inherit unconscious pre-images and psychic structures descended from generation to generation. Archetypes provide the base of behavior, structuralization of the self of a person, world understanding, inner unity and relation between culture and sympathy.

Archiving 891001 89819 – structuring and information management in long time memory.

Asymmetry 519064 08918 – symmetry absence or disorder.

Interhemispheric asymmetry 418718391 488 – the characteristic of arrangement of psychic functions between left and right hemispheres: when producing of some functions the lead is left hemisphere, it is the right one corresponding to others.

Asynchrony 519718314 812 – the characteristic of the processes, not coinciding in time.

© Grabovoi G.P., 2003

31

Austerity 498714 819 – antic notion means preparation of athletes for sport contests. Then it has got wide interpretation and now is interpreted as the struggle with sins and drive to virtuous life.

Assimilation 419712 819 – mechanism, providing the application of earlier accepted skills under new conditions without their essential change, by means of which a new object or a situation join with amount of objects or with other situations, for which the scheme already exists.

Associanism 548714 3198 01 – one of the direction of world psychological idea explicative towards the psychic processes dynamics by the principle of association.

Association 591 482 891098 – the linkage between psychic phenomena, formed under certain conditions for which the actualization (perception, representation) of one of them involves the appearance of another one. Psychophysiologic base of association is acquired reflex. In social psychology it is the group where there is no mutual activity, organization and management, at that value orientations indirectly showing the interpersonal relations are displayed under conditions of group communication.

Astasia 918008 969314 – disturbance of ability to stand, caused by disorder of body muscles coordination as a result of wide damages of frontal sections and callosum.

Asthenic 555 8910198 45 – an individual with the following peculiarities of body: slim build, narrow shoulders and chest, long legs, pale face, long and thin nose. Asthenia patient has as a rule schizoid or schizotypal temperament, characterized by unsociable behavior, exposing an incoherence of backward reactions to outer stimuli, high sensitivity at emotional frigidity and experience of asthenic susceptibilities.

Asthenia 456 891 01 2139 – 1. Neuropsychic syndrome expressed as high fatigability, exhaustion, low threshold of perception, extremely unstable mood and disturbance of sleep. It appears as the result of various diseases, excessive mental and physical overstrain and durable negative feelings and conflicts. 2. Specific attribute of a character. 2 types such as asthenic and psychasthenic are related to the asthenic group. Their common features are high sensitivity and fast exhaustion. They are excitable and exhausting in neuropsychic sense.

Astereognosis 531 488914 019 – the type of tactile agnosia which is revealed in impossibility to recognize familiar objects by tactile probing with closed eyes. It is caused by the damage of secondary cortical zones of parietal region of cortex, leading to reduction of tactile images of objects and to the disorder of analysis and synthesis of different skin-kinesthetic perception, coming to the cerebral parietal area when one touches an object.

Astrology 489717 319481 – Ancient theory about the influence of cosmic objects on earth life included fate and human behavior.

Atavism 891012 31978014 – manifestation of some features of an organism in the period of its growth, inherited from its far ancestors, because previously these features had played an important adaptive role, what has been lost later.

Brainstorming 318319 489 061 – technique of stimulation of creative activity and productiveness.

Attribution 918919 818 714 – attachment to social objects (a person, a group, social community) the characteristics not represented in the field of perception. Attribution is the main way of additional construction of direct perceptible information. Attribution is considered as the mechanism of many social processes; its role in intergroup interaction, in regulation of marital relations, in appearing of business conflicts and etc. was shown in domestic social psychology.

Causal attribution 498714318712 – interpretation by a man of interpersonal perception of causes and motives of other people behavior.

Atrophy 314812 819714 – degeneration of organic structure. In terms of psychology it is used in the meaning of degeneration of some psychic function caused by not-training or unfavorable traumatic actions sort of long stress, conflicts, frustration, drugs, intoxication and etc.

Attraction 314819 719 579 – the concept, meaning the appearance of attractiveness of one person for another when one person perceiving by another.

Audience 319481919241 – In terms of psychology a group, perceiving speech. It is usually a disposed in space little group, united by interaction with a communicator in the process of perception of announcement speech.

Autism 428 516 319017 – concept defines the extreme form and psychological estrangement state, expressed as detachment, recession, escape of the individual from contacts with reality and in immersion in reserved world of idiotropic type behavior, when voluntary arrangement of thinking is damaged because of its submission to affective needs.

Infantile autism 428 516 3190 – child or teenager's feature, development of which characterizes by sharp reduction of contacts with neighborhood, badly developed speech and specific reaction to changes in surroundings.

Early infantile autism 428 516 319017 491 – clinic syndrome the main features of which are an inborn inability to establish affective contact with the help of a glance, facial expressions and gestures, but not caused by low intellectual level; stereotypic behavior, unusual reactions to stimuli, frustration of speech development, early appearance (till 30th month of life).

Aphasia 491819 319 812 – full or partial loss of speech ability; speech disorder, appearing associated with local damages of the left hemisphere of cortex (for right-hand). It is the system disorder of speech activity of various types expressed as speech comprehension and disturbance of phonemic, morphological and syntax structure of speech, when the motions of speech apparatus and elementary forms of hearing are remained.

Aphony 519 317 919 064819 - loss of voice when the wholeness of speech is retained. It appears as organic and functional disorders of larynx (vocal, larynx muscles) for instance as a result of over-tension of lecturer's larynx muscles as well as of sudden strong excitements or hysteria.

Affect 598071 319498 – strong and approximately short-time neuropsychic excitement, emotional state associated with sharp change of important for the person's life circumstances. It is accompanied with sharp expressed movement appearance and changes in functions of internal organs, loss of willing control and display of emotions. It appears as a response to already happened event and if it is kind of shifted to its end. Affect is developing under critical conditions when the patient is unable to find adequate way out from dangerous, often unexpected situations.

Affect: accumulation 8071 319498 918 – the process of prolonged accumulation of negative emotions of low force with further discharge as stormy and practically uncontrolled affective explosion, approaching without visible reasons.

Inadequacy affect 071 319498 489 – negative emotional state, appearing in response to lack of success, failure. It is characterized with either negation of the fact of failure or replace of responsibility for it on others. It may be displayed in high offensiveness, suspicious, aggressiveness and negativism.

Affective 319 814518017 – belongs to the state of pleasure or displeasure associated with sensations, emotions, feelings and thoughts.

Afference 459 714 899 081 – constant flow of nervous impulses, entering the cerebral nervous system from sensory organs which perceive information either from external stimuli (exteroception) or internal organs (interoception). It is directly depending on the force of stimuli and their intenseness in the environment and also on the state of activeness or passiveness of an individual.

Afference changed 314571089384 – specific reaction of an organism in case of sharp changes, unfamiliar living conditions. It is drastically displayed under the null-gravity influence and when afference relatively otholitic apparatus,

© Grabovoi G.P., 2003

locomotor apparatus, cardiovascular and other systems is sharply changed. For patient, which experiences null-gravity for the first time it appears a sense of falling down accompanied with negative emotions.

Afferent 498741 818 299 – the characteristic of centripetence of the processes of nervous stimulation, their direction along the nervous system from the periphery to the center, in particular, to the cortex.

Affiliation 591 394 818 544 – need to be in human society, need for communication and realization of emotional contacts, for appearance of friendship and love.

_Б_

Barbiturate dependence 498714 319888 - type of toxic mania. It is characterized by need for accepting of barbiturates.

Psychological barrier 498714 889057 - psychic state, displaying as inadequate inertness, preventing the fulfillment of these and that actions, inner obstacle of psychological nature: lack of desire, fear, uncertainty etc. In social behavior psychological barriers are expressed by communicative barriers, revealing absence of empathy, rigidness of interpersonal social norms and etc. as well as semantic barriers.

Semantic barrier 598 069 49812 - mutual misunderstanding among people, appearing when communicating, because the participants of communication assign different meaning to one and the same event and see different motivation in their depth.

Escape in disease 591398 712 889 - a notion and conception, fixing and explaining reasons and mechanisms of a set of psychic diseases, especially neurosis characterized by presence of unconscious person's strive to diseases and escape in illness as the mean and way of defense from a conflict and reality.

Escape from freedom 498881019781 - a notion and conception, fixing and explaining reasons and mechanisms of the action of dynamic factors of psyche, stimulating a person to willingly deny freedom.

Counseling 51931791419 891 in psychology a method to receive an information on basis of verbal communication which refers to questioning method.

Clinical counseling 51931791419 018 - the method to receive an information by means of questioning of a client and carrying out of therapeutic counseling with giving of psychological, psychiatry and medical care.

Learned helplessness 519371 818911 -the state arising when a person or animals experience a rather prolonged aversive influence, which is impossible to avoid. Animals' learned helplessness is manifested in motion inhibition, reduction of biological motivations, disturbance of ability to gain new habits, also as various somatic disorders e.g. hair fall, high blood pressure, ulcer of mucous membrane of gastrointestinal tract, reduction of general resistance of the organism etc. Learned helplessness for person is expressed by emotional disorders (depression or neurotic anxiety) and possible appearance of psychosomatic disorders.

Cognitive helplessness 519891319488 - psychological state or situation, as a result of which the person having acquired necessary knowledge, skills for solving the tasks, becomes unable to solve them because of a reasons' set.

Unconscious 591008 719311 - 1. Complex of psychic processes, acts and states, caused by phenomena of reality, in relation to which there is no subjective conscious control and the individual is not aware of influence of which. It will occur to be unconscious what does not become the matter of special conscious actions. 2. The form of psychic reflection in which the image of reality and person's attitude to it are not the matter of special reflection and comprise an integral whole.

Absolute unconscious 519 377898 997 (super conscious) superior senses and abilities, intuition, inspiration.

Collective unconscious 7898 898 742 - special form

of social being of unconscious as the accumulator, bearer and storage of genetic inherited experience of phylogenetic development of mankind.

Personal unconscious 318 482 55946192 – it is formed in the process of development of personal experience of the man and comprises content ousted from by him/her which appears to be complexes.

Inferior unconscious 598 484 558 7191 - instinctive motives, passions, primitive desires and etc.

Social unconscious 428 01916 559 89014213- unconscious, typical for most of people, ousted elements, the content of which is what the given society does not allow its members to get across to conscious if it is going to act successfully further on the base of its contradictions.

Unconscious middle 8819905191714213 – thoughts and senses which may be comprehended easily.

Unconsciousness 489 091319611 – one of psychological distinctions which appears to be not characteristic though.

Beater 591319 811 799 – ethno specific term, meaning the form of psychotherapy, used in folk medicine of Madagascar, directed to the harmony of self-estimation of a weak person, obsessed by neurotic symptoms.

Biologism 429 312 918 542 - one of the reason which behaviorism made relation to when rejecting to study consciousness, was the lack of information on corresponding neuromechanisms. Past science position did not allow to make objective approach to the research of the cortex role in phenomena of consciousness.

Biopsychism 489712 819 32281 - the theory in natural sciences, according to which the psyche is ascribed to all alive including plants.

Evolutional biopsychology 891498 719 422 - psychology comparative and zoo- are often united in the discipline.

Biophile 319 415888 78219 - a person or type of the person focused on love for all alive and on creation.

Contradicting notion is necrophile.

Biophilia 498 889 317428 - (biophilic positioning) one type of general basic positioning defined life pattern and expressed by affection towards life and all living with intention to love, to create and to bonify.

Bioenergy 918714 -the main aim of the therapy is to return a person to his 'primary nature' i.e. the state of sincere satisfaction, released motions, release of his body and man's involvement in life. 'Return to body' is implemented by means of special exercises based on tension and relaxation of certain groups of muscles and also on verbal ways of detained emotions' release.

Bisexuality 591488989784 - (bisexual predisposition) dual sexuality is the notion, reflecting dual nature of sexuality, caused by presence in each individual of male and female elements, the certain type of sex preferences and behavior is formed depending on development and balance of which.

Behaviorism 918491519 318 – the branch of American psychology of 20th ctr. It was forming as the discipline with distinct natural scientific focusing. The founders were trying to find forms of the objective approach to psychic life. According to behaviorism such notions as consciousness, sensations, suffering etc. cannot be considered as scientific, because as the result of self-examination they are subjective and cannot be fixed by non-prejudicial scientific means. The matter of research may be behavior and activity. Activity external or internal is described by means of the notion of reaction related to which the sort of organism changes might be which could be feasibly recorded.

Dizygotic twins 591848 - twins, developing from 2 different zygotes of simultaneous fertilization by 2 different spermatozoids. There may be of the same or different gender and reveal the same differences that usual brothers and sisters do.

Closeness 399016488 917- type of situation including two persons and giving the possibilities to establish personal values on the base of cooperation, that is conveyed by

© Grabovoi G.P., 2003

mutual adaptive behavior, aimed at achievement of growing mutual satisfaction and sense of safety of own position.

Brain divisions 489 718916314 - structural-functional model of cerebral localization of higher psychic functions of a person.

Bovarism 591 318 719488 - the term means clinic state, characterized by loss of ability to draw the distinct line between reality and fancy, inclination to substitute the real by illusive. But fancy world may have either positive valence or negative one (fantasy of fear).

Wakefulness 48931748519 – the other way it is active state. It is traditionally considered in west psychology as the state of activation of organism integrally, allowing it to catch, to select and to interpret external signals, to send some of them in memory or to respond to them adequately or inadequately depending on prior experience and skills.

Disease 548764319 017 - quite practical summary concept, means the threshold of summing of predisposition and sensation, as the result of which many people pass from the group of healthy to the type of psychopathic or vice versa.

Down disease (trisomy 21) 519517819 31 -inborn anomaly conditioned by presence of additional, 3rd chromosome 21 (the other name is coming from). Patients differ with mongoloid face features and mild debility.

Pain 498712891319 - psychic state, appearing as a result of over powerful or destructive influences on organism menaced for its existence or wholeness.

Fear (phobia) 891 019 4918808 - state of waiting of a danger and preparedness for it.

Delirium (phenomenon delirious) 8142351 - forming as a result of a disease, constellation of different images, reasoning, ideas, thoughts, non-correspondent to reality no one can reassure about which.

Bureaucracy 498712 818914 - in terms of psychology the phenomenon, appearing under conditions of economical ties between faceless administrative apparatus and social object and excluding the impact by people on this apparatus. Administrative apparatus, turning in cohesive elite, opposes to any social changes or try to be adapted to them, preserving the control lever (key factor). It may be revealed at any level of functioning of social structure: at the level of organizations and prime subdivisions. Its main features are rigid regimentation of behavior and ways of transmittance of information at all levels of control and fulfillment, conformism, authoritarianism of consciousness. It demands from the person the indisputable acceptance of existing order of things, absence of own position, following the prescribed model uncritically, keeping of 'psychological distance' between controlling elite and subordinates. In social and psychological sense it is expressed also as resistance to innovations, personal initiative, creative search, propagation of incompetence and careerism.

_B_

Validity 519317418 914 - one of the most important features of psychodiagnostics techniques and tests, one of the basic criteria of their quality. This notion is close to the notion of credibility, but not quite identical. Validity points to what exactly the test method measures and how good it does it; the more it valid the better it reflects the quality for which it was created.

Validity: criterion 317418 914498 - applying to techniques it means independent marks and parameters, according to which it is possible to judge about its validity. According to these criteria the results, received in practical application are estimated. Criteria can be: behavior marks that are reactions, actions of a testee in different life situation; his achievements in different kinds of activity such as study, labor etc; data on the fulfillment of various control tasks; data received from other methods, validity or the connection of which with tested method is considered to be firmly established.

Validity external 418914498 5941 - means applying

to psychodiagnostic methods correspondence of the results of psychodiagnostics carrying out by the given technique, to independent from the technique external attributes that refer to the subject of the research. It means approximately the same as validity empirical, the difference is however that here we talk about the connection between the marks of the technique and the most important key external attributes assigned to the testee behavior. Psychodiagnostic method is considered to be externally valid if, for example, by its mean the individual's features of character are estimated and his externally observed behavior corresponds to the result of the carried out test.

Validity internal 319481 5941 418 - means applying to psychodiagnostic methods correlation of the included in it tests, subtests and etc. with the general aim of the method; correlation of the result of psychodiagnostics, carrying out by its mean, to the definition of the estimated psychic feature used in the method. The technique is considered internally not valid or not sufficiently valid when all or part of the questions, tasks or subtests, inserted in it, measure otherwise than what is required by this technique.

Conceptional validity 4184498 59 41 819 - is understood as the ground relative to correlation of author apprehensions about peculiarities of the testing feature, as the measure of correlation of test's tasks to the author conception of these features.

Criterial validity 4198914498 31 (validity by criteria). It is interpreted as the ground of correlation between test's results and empiric criteria. The correlation of the test to the criteria points to the possible validity of the test in relation to that criterion; the higher the coefficient of correlation the higher is the validity. Development of the factor analysis helped to create tests valid in the relation to the identification factor.

Validity theoretical 419898914498 (constructive validity or conceptual validity) - applicable to psychodiagnostic techniques it means correlation of the result of psychic diagnosis through this technique to the appropriate indicators of the psychological qualities that are theoretically related to the assessed property. It is determined by the conformity of quality produced by this methodology as that obtained by other methods or at their theoretically sound dependence.

Validity empirical 891419898914498 (validity practical) - applicable to psychodiagnostic techniques it means correlation of the result of psychodiagnosis through this technique to the experience of man, his actual behavior and observed actions and reactions of the subject. It is determined by comparing its performance with real-life behavior or results of practical activity of people.

Vampire 519418 719 314 - an image of a corpse, sucking blood from sleeping people. Haunting of the patient's imagination and often met in clinic and psychoanalytical practice it expresses the patient's visualization of the sensations as if all his psychic power is taken away by somebody other.

Inspiration 891498314 719 - the state of specific tension and raising of spiritual forces, creative excitement of a person, leading to the appearance and realization of intention and idea of a performance of science, art, techniques. Typical are high general activity, unusual productiveness of enterprise, consciousness of ease of creation, sensation of obsession and emotional immersion in creation.

Vegetotherapy 591061718 489 - type of therapy body-oriented. The main methods of vegetotherapy are connected to massage and breathing and also motion and vocal exercises of different types.

Belief 598 888 998 617 -1.Special state of human psyche, consisting in full and undisputable acceptance of some information, texts, phenomena, events or own purposes and thoughts, which in the future can become the ground of his 'ego', define some of his acts, reasoning, standard of behavior and relations. 2. Acceptance that something is the truth, with such resolution, that exceeds the force of external

© Grabovoi G.P., 2003

actual and formal logical arguments.

Verbal 514381 914 811 - it is the term for the definition of forms of sign material and also the processes of operation with this material in terms of psychology.

Verification 519481 719 311 — when checking of scientific concepts it is a proof or other convincing demonstration of that the phenomena, included in the volume and content of the given notion, really exist and correlate to the certain notion. It supposes the presence of the experimental method of the test of the phenomenon, describing by the notion. The check is carried out by means of correspondent psychodiagnostic procedures.

Substance 5193618901 - neuromodular serving for transmission of pain signals within nervous system.

Interaction 589017942891 — the process in terms of psychology of direct and indirect impact of object (subject) one on another, generating their interdependence and ties. It acts as the integrating factor useful for the formation of structures.

Interaction of analyzers 7942891489 - one of the manifestations of the unity of sensory sphere. Interaction reveals itself also in common work of analyzers, giving the subject the information about sides of outer world, about which no one analyzer of its own gives (e.g. binocular estimation of remoteness of an object when operating together of visual and proprioceptive analyzer).

Group interaction 51431458948189 – the process of direct or indirect influence of multiple objects (subjects) on each other, generating their mutual determination and ties; takes place among parts of groups and among the whole groups. It acts as integrating factor useful when generating of structures. Structure of groups reveals as status relations, group aims and values and performances of accepted by all members of the group standard of behavior and interactions.

Interpersonal interaction 4589481948 31798 – 1) In wide sense it is occasional or intentional, private or public, long-time or short-time, verbal or nonverbal personal contact of two or more people, involving interchanges of their behavior, activity, relations and attitudes. Such interpretation is usually used to point to the direct interconnection of interacting individuals. 2) In a strict sense it is the system of mutually determined individual actions, connected with cyclic causal dependence, at that the behavior of each of participants is the stimulus and the reaction to the behavior of all the rest at the same time.

Psychological interaction 591489 316 - from the materialistic perspective it is the idealistic approach to psychological problem, according to which consciousness and its nervous (body) substrate are two inter influencing independent sources.

In-group expert estimation 398716914 816 - the social and psychological method based on the estimation of various personal and interpersonal characteristics through the way of cross questioning of the group members, which play the role of experts evaluating each other's behavior in important situations of communication and common activity.

Mutual understanding: mechanism 314821069 711 – the following identification, reflection, representativeness and also the mechanism of feedback.

Vivation 914891319 – the modification of Rebirthing is typical for focusing on the exercising with senses, appearing in altered states of consciousness. It is performed on the base of 5 elements: 1st is worked out in details of the breathing techniques; 2nd is the technique of achievement of full relaxation; 3rd combines the methods of deep relaxation, oriented to any inner states (physical senses, emotions, image); 4th is based on the search of the context in which negative senses will not be suppressed, but accepted with joy and benevolence; 5th is the self-belief and trust in a physician.

Vivation: breathing type 9144891319 317 – special breathing exercises, supporting the achievement of altered states of consciousness and operation in the position with inner reality.

Biological species 519519 – complex of genetically

© Grabovoi G.P., 2003

similar species capable to intrabreed and give fruitful descendants.

Guilt: source 23940191967 1 (2 sources of guilt) – the source of sense of guilt is fear that is transformed into conscience later.

Taste 498756714 217 - one of the types of chemoreception revealed the sensitivity of the receptors of oral cavity toward chemical irritants. It is subjectively revealed as gustative senses – bitter, sour, sweet, salted and their combinations. Taste contrast may appear as alteration of a set of chemical substances (after salt water may seem to be sweet). The whole taste image appears as a result of interaction of taste, tactile, temperature and osmetic receptors.

Attraction 219317 919 89 is instinctive desire, inducing an individual to act towards satisfaction of this desire. Psychic state, expressing undifferentiated unconscious or not sufficiently conscious need for a subject having already sense-feeling but not yet connected to making it conscious aims.

Attraction: source 231489 487 51 - the somatic process of some organ or part of body excitation of which is embodied in attraction for spiritual sphere.

Attraction: limitation 918 817 - caused by society process of defining of conditions and limits of manifestation of conjugate aggressive and erotic inclinations.

Attraction: fixation 489136019 -the stoppage and fixation of an attraction, especially private, at some level, stage, phase, period of development.

Attraction retarded 48719 31917 - drives, inhibited on the way to satisfaction of an active or passive aim, as the result of which the long-time affection to the object and resistant strive are appeared, e.g., caressing relationship.

Attraction to life 888999 719 421 – (life instinct) – provides preservation, support and development of life in all aspects.

Attraction to death 319 460 6169 (thanatos) that is

specific anti-social contrast to the drive to life. It inserts the tendencies to self-destruction and return to inorganic state which reveals aggression to persons and objects. Opposition to eternal development may be openly or hidden carried out by individuals, having the drive to death.

Primary attraction 515 519 814913 – inseparable, elementary attractions.

Sexual attraction 498516719 311 – multi meaning term, denoting either sex appeal in general or the striving to body closeness with a certain person, and motivational aspect of sexuality.

Sex appeal 548711 918 211 (eros, sexual instinct) –the irritating force originating from inner sources and aimed at the elimination of sexual excitement through direct or indirect satisfaction of primary urges. It predetermines and corresponds to the need of love and acts as the drive to life.

Influence 598417 398 411 –the process and the result in terms of psychology towards changing of the behavior of other person, his intentions, purposes, values and etc. by an individual in the process of interaction.

Individual specific influence 319481 919811 - the form of personalization, realized due to the translation to other people of own personal features in form of not yet acquired by them models of personal activity. It leads to the gradual transformation of personal senses, behavior and motivational sphere of other people, manifested in essential change of their activity in the moment of conscious actualization of the image of an individual that is the subject of influence. This type of influence explains the principle of the set of phenomena of social facilitation and realizes either as purposeful activity (learning, educational measures and etc.) or as any other cases of interaction of personality as the subject of influence on other people.

Functional role influence 317 814891444 - type of influence, character, intensiveness and targeting of which are not defined by personal peculiarities of partners in interaction, but their role positions.

© Grabovoi G.P., 2003

Infatuation 515889 - the feeling and state, which are grounded on the base of direct and (in sense of aim) inhibited sexual strivings, so as the object of infatuation pulls over the part of narcissistic libido of an ego. The essence of infatuation lies in narcissistic libido change into the libido aimed at an object. Its power is ample to eliminate repressions and restore perversions. It lifts the sexual object up to the level of sexual ideal.

Attention 391118918714 - a subject activity focusing on some real or ideal object such as thing, event, image etc. at a time. Attention is the dynamic side of consciousness, characterizing the degree of its targeting at the object and focusing on it with the aim to provide adequate reflection in the course of time necessary for performance of a certain act or communication. It is evident as selective reflection of objects, corresponding to the subject's needs, aims and tasks of his activity.

Attention: volume 505 641719 317 - one of the feature of attention, showing what amount of objects can be perceived or what amount of actions can be performed simultaneously. The most habitual experimental model for research of volume of attention is the definition of the volume of perception depended on exposition time; character of stimulating material and individual's skills. So, when visual stimuli exposing during 0.1 sec the average volume of attention equals 7+\-2 objects. Whether generalization of perceivable objects is possible the volume of attention significantly increases.

External attention 598716 319811 (sensory perceptive attention). It turns to objects of outer world. It is to be the necessary condition of cognition and transformation of outer world.

Inner attention (intellectual) 498716319817 – turns to objects of subjective world of a person. It is to be necessary condition of self cognition and self education.

Involuntary attention 519489 319716 is of the simplest and genetic origin. It is showing its inactive nature

48 © Grabovoi G.P., 2003

while imposed to the subject by outer events relatively to its activity aims. It happens to be independently supported by conscious intentions, due to peculiarities of an object such as novelty, impact, correspondence to actual need and etc. Physiological manifestation of this type of attention is orientative reaction.

Post voluntary attention 519310219611 . It appears to be based on voluntary attention and consists of focusing on an object due to its value, importance or interest for a personality. Its occurrence is possible in course of development of operational-technical side activity connected to its automation and transition of actions into operation, and also as a result of motivation changes (shift of a motive towards an aim). Psychic tension is released and conscious attention targeting is perceived, as well as correspondence of the aimed activity to the accepted aims, but its performance does not require special mental efforts and limited in time only by tiredness and exhaustion of organism resources.

Voluntary attention 879491488711 – It is targeted and supported by the aim put consciously and then tightly connected to speech. It is said of voluntary attention if the activity is carried out in the frame of conscious intentions and demands volitional forces from a subject. It characterizes by activity, complex structure, indirect organization of behavior and communication by socially elaborated ways; it indigenously is connected to industrial activity.

Suggestibility 594321714 811 – the measure or the degree of susceptibility to suggestion, increased suppleness to the promptings, provoked by other people, are defined and limited by several factors, mainly the subjective willingness to undergo and submit inspires impact. Uncritical acceptance of someone else's point of view and a willingness to submit to (obey), when a person changes their behavior with an explicit statement of the respective legal authority. Propensity to undergo of strangers impact and learn from other people's moods habits. Characteristic of the individual depends on situational and personal factors.

© Grabovoi G.P., 2003

Suggestion 598712814314 – goal-seeking process of immediate or indirect impact on the psychic sphere of a person and on the performance of the suggested content. It is associated with low consciousness and criticalness when perceiving and realizing of the suggested content, and also with absence of purposeful active attention, wide logical analysis and estimation together with former experience and given state of the subject.

Post-hypnotic suggestion 319481 918 the phenomenon of behavior, when a task taken by a person being hypnotic then indisputably is performed by him being awaken so that the fact of task existence is not known.

Excitability 548 312688 7 - the characteristic of living creatures to become excited under influence of irritants or stimuli with preservation of its traits for some time.

Excitement 591 016 718 - the feature of living creatures as an active response of the agitated tissue to stimulation. It's the main function of nervous system. Cells forming it tend to conduct the irritation from sections where it happened to other sections and to neighbor cells. Because of that nervous cells are able to transmit signals from one structures of an organism to another, so the excitement becomes the carrier of information of characteristics coming from outside irritants and together with inhibition it is the regulator of activity of all organs and systems of the organism.

Traumatic excitement 591489 318 716 – external irritations, rather strong to break the defense from irritation and to overfill psychic system with great amount of irritants, influencing the psychics traumatically.

Influence 519617489 –psychological term for purposeful transfer of motion and information from one member of interaction to other one.

Influence abiotic (biologically neutral influence) 319 – those types of energy or features of the objects which do not immediately involved in metabolism. They are not useful or harmful in themselves.

Age 489712618488 —Psychological category denoted qualitatively specific step of ontogenetic development or temporal features of individual development (chronological age, psychological age).

Age pre-school 5487123196 18 – the stage of psychic development of children aged 3 through 6-7 years. Typical is that key activity is a game. It is very important for formation of child's personality.

Age babyhood 5419 – the period of child's life from his birth to 1st year.

Age adolescence 5289149 316 – the period of ontogenesis (of children aged 10-11 through 15 years) corresponding to the transmittance from childhood to youth.

Age psychological 81842171482631 – contrary to chronological age the notion means certain specific stage of ontogenetic development, determined by regularities of forming of an organism by life conditions, education and teaching and having particular historical origin.

Early age 408 712 – the stage of psychic development of a child aged 1 through 3 years. Qualitative changes in development of function of cerebrum hemispheres are typical.

Age mental 319 744 818 914 – the notion of characterization of the intellectual development on the base of its comparison with intellectual level of other people of the same age. The age for which such test tasks are solved, that are acceptable for a testee at an average, is expressed quantitatively.

Age chronological 488 728 913 - expresses the duration of an individual's existence from the moment of birth.

Junior-school age 513489614 - the period of life of a child aged 6-7 through 10 years, when he/she is learning at primary school (1-4 forms).

Adolescence Age 489 712 814 212 – the stage of ontogenetic development between adolescent age and adultness. For youngster it includes the period 17 through 21 years, for young girls aged 16 through 20 years. At the age the physical, sexual maturation of an organism finishes. In terms of psychology the main feature of the age is the join the self-consistent life, when they choose an occupation and social position is sharply changed.

Voluntarism 598716 917481 – the branch in terms of psychology and philosophy, admitting a will as the specific, over nature power, put on the ground of psyche and existence on the whole. It reveals itself as the establishment of the will as the prime ability, determined only by a subject and defines all other psychic processes and phenomena. Inherent ability of a person of independent choice of an aim and ways of its achievement, ability to make decision, expressing his individual attitudes and reasoning, voluntarism interprets as the effect of the action of specific irrational spiritual self.

Will (volition) 513964 818 91 – the side of consciousness, its active and regulative origin, assigned to create the effort and keep it as long as it is necessary. A person's ability to achieve his aims under conditions of overcoming circumstances, revealing self-determination and self-regulation of own activity and various psychic processes. Thanks to it a person can perform actions by his own initiative, coming out from conscious necessity, in planned in advance direction and with foreseen power.

Will irrational 898716 074819 – irrational passions and strivings, obsessing and subordinating a person, who cringingly realizes uncontrolled impulses.

Will rational 519317919 817 – purposeful, realistic, control behavior and energetic efforts, aimed at achievement of a rational objective.

Imagination 348716814916 – man's ability to construct new images by processing of psychic components, acquired through previous experience; psychic process of creation of objects' image or situation through reconstruction of existing visualizations. The part of person's consciousness, one of the cognitive processes, characterized by high degree of visualization and concretion. In imagination external world is reflected specifically and singularly, image anticipation of results goes, the results that can be achieved by means of these and those actions; it allows to program not only future behavior but imagine possible conditions under which the behavior will be realized.

Imagination active 31705689 9889 – there are 2 types: creative and reconstructive imagination.

Imagination reconstructive 531784911674 – open on the ground of description, story, scheme, symbol or a sign. It is based on the creation of any particular images, corresponding to the description. A person fills the original material with the images he has.

Imagination passive 314812488712 – characterized by creation of images which are not embodied in life: programs that are not carried out or in general cannot be fulfilled. Imagination acts as the substitution of an activity, its surrogate, because of which a person refuses to act.

Imagination creative 52196107074312 – It supposes independent creation of an image, object, feature, having no analogous; realized in original and valuable products of activity.

Upbringing 548712684212 - the activity for transfer of social-historical experience to new generations; planned and purposeful influence, the consciousness and behavior of a man with the aim to form certain attitudes, notions, principles, value orientation, providing the conditions for its development, preparedness for social life and work.

Recall (recollection) 518471818211 – extracting from long-time memory the images of the past, reproduction of events of life, mentally located in time and space.

Screen recollection 51831791848 – secondary child's recalls which, when remembered, act in place of primary, creating the view of less meaningfulness of the former. They are produced as the result of shift in reproduction and substitute the drive, ousted in unconscious, with which they are bound in association and if they cover it.

© Grabovoi G.P., 2003

Recollection voluntary 534961784421 – in voluntary recall of some event the relation to it is reconstructed consciously, that may be accompanied by corresponding to the event emotions.

Perception 519714984217 – the whole reflection of things, phenomena, situations and events in their sense accessible temporal and space ties and relations; the process of formation – by means of active actions – of subjective image of a whole object, immediately influencing on the analysers. It is determined by the fact that the world of phenomena tends to be presentive. It appears as direct impact of physical irritants on the sensory organs' receptor surfaces. Together with process of sensation it provides direct sense orientation in external world.

Perception: operational denomination 31948801691812 (operational denomination of perception) – Some location in perceptive separate objects field corresponds to operational perception unites. The content of these unites is changed In the process of activity development. So when learning of telegraph code every separate unite, dot or slash, is perceived as independent unite. Then there do the longer consequence of telegraph signs as letters, words, even word combinations. The transfer to the more large operational unites of perception based on the sense combination, communication or recoding of informational elements allows increasing of the speed of perception.

Perception; process: ontogenesis 519488 – (perception process ontogenesis) pattern changes, going during perception in the course of individual development. The main factor responsible for the construction of adequate perceptive practice is the practical actions such as activity for transformation of the objects of external world.

Perception: development 59148871931 2189 – qualitative alteration of perception with the growth of the body and the accumulation of individual experience, its process and result

Perception: type 514817914997 – type of perception, characterizes mainly introverted or extraverted tendencies of the personality. Types of perception correlate with certain components of an intellect, dynamics affective, features of a character and types of psychic pathology.

Perception visual 6386617189118 – complex of processes of construction of an image visual of outer world.

Perception visual: micro genesis 514919314999 – successive phases of visual image construction, beginning from space and temporal localization of the object of perception till the emphasis of some particularities in it.

Intergroup perception 548712612777 – process of social perception, in which subject and object of perception are groups or social communities. It is characterized by stereotype, more cohesion of cognitive and emotional components, bright affective coloring and sharply expressed estimating targeting.

Perception interpersonal 549316999816 – perception, understanding and evaluation of one another.

Perception subliminal (unconscious) 598516019711 – object perception, realizing without conscious control: phenomenon, when information overcomes psychological threshold but does not achieve the threshold of conscious perception. In influences an organism and able to call the backward reaction.

Perception subconscious 531718914 – the form of direct reflection of psychic reality, caused by such irritants, the influence of which the subject is unconscious; one of the manifestations of unconscious. Unconscious perception and processing of signals, coming through sensory organs and not achieving the threshold.

Perception haptic 219481719311 – one of the forms of mechanoreceptors' perception. Sensory system, responsible for construction of tactile image in haptic perception, consists of skin analysers and kinesthetic ones. The construction of tactile image is determined by tactile movement of a hand, and so the contour of an object is reproduces.

Reproduction procedure (recall) 489406918766 – the process of extraction of information from long-time memory – actualization of early formed psychological content (thoughts, images, senses, movements) under condition of absence of actually perceiving indicators.

Recall involuntary 498714819317 – observed in situation when a thought or an image show as memory without personal volition; when there is no specially put tasks of reproduction and it appears under the influence of notions, thoughts and senses, called by perception of some objects or situation or activity, performing at the given moment – reading a book, seeing a film etc.

Recall voluntary 319716064817 – caused by a task of reproduction of something, preservation in long-time memory, that is put for oneself or by other people. May occur at the level of recognition.

Restoration 319712419888891 – (reflex restoration) inhibition i.e. partial or full restoration of conditional reflex after slackening of it or after time break (spontaneous restoration) or as the result of appearance of unconditional again stimuli or supporting agent of the reflex.

Susceptibility 498714816 - the ability to have presentations, different in brightness and in connection with outer world, with different degree of expression of senses in them. This quality of personality is derived from representations.

Warming-up 598712488212 – the process of adaptation to the actually activity, in the time of which the arrangement of all psychophysiologic functions occur at the expense of actualization of dynamic stereotype. The excitement and functional movability of nervous system increases, concentration of stimulation of nervous processes increases also. Such arrangement leads to the decreasing in time of operations performance, to increase of rhythmic work and its productiveness. Warming-up usually finishes in first hours of work and after that the constant working state comes.

Time 519641888910219 – in terms of psychology an object of multiple theoretic and experimental researches, the main aspects of which are 1) psychophysical as the research of mechanism of reflection of psychic topological (sequence, simultaneous) and metric (duration) features of physical time; 2) psycho-physiological as the research of influence of bio-rhythms of different levels and regularities of organization of "biological" time on the dynamics of psychic processes; 3) social-psychological as consideration of peculiarities of reflection by a person the social time, the specific of this reflection in different communities and cultural-historical conditions; 4) personal-psychological as research of temporal organization of individual life way, structure of physiological time of personality.

Time: perception 591489317899 12 – image reflection of such features of phenomena and processes of internal reality as duration, speed and sequence. When building of time aspects of world picture different analysers take part; among which the kinesthetic and auditory senses play most important role in precise differentiation of time intervals. Individual perception of the duration of time periods essentially depends on intensiveness of activity and on emotional states, originating in the process of activity.

Time: perception: violation 516788918 317 – (disorders of time perception) – loss of ability of time orienting.

Time psychological 521489 317989 – psyche reflection of the system of temporal relations between events of life way.

Reaction time – 4897163197668 – time interval between presentation stimuli i.e. some signals (optic, acoustic, tactile etc.) and the beginning of testee response determined by an instructions towards this signal.

Recall 498712819 3 – the process of extraction of information from memory.

Voyeurism 591489 319611 – sexual deviation i.e.

substitution of sexual life by secret spying after sexual act or genitals organs.

Choice interpersonal: motivation 517914817214 – the system of motives, producing the psychological ground of individual preference. The analysis of motivation of interpersonal choices allows to define the psychological causes, according to them an individual is ready to realize emotional and business contact with one member of a group and reject other.

Sampling 498712688522 – a group of testees, representing the certain population and selected for experiment and research. Opposite notion is general constellation. Sampling is the part of general constellation.

Sampling dependent 534981 914891 – samples, consisting of results of one and the same test after two or more different impacts.

Sampling representative 591644311814 891 – sampling performed according to rules, so that it reflects the specific of general constellation either in composition or individual features of inserting object.

Advantage secondary 498716519388 -by illness: 1) use of situation of illness by self-preservation instinct and ego for acquiring of certain benefits, material or psychological; 2) real or suggested advantages and privileges acquired by a patient in result of pathogenic symptoms or illness.

Avenging 498716388517 – specific form of projection i.e. unconscious reorientation of an impulse or sense for the more accessible object.

Repression 59871798139 – one of the type of psychological defense – the process as the result of which unacceptable for an individual thoughts, recalls, drives, senses are replaced from consciousness and transferred into the sphere of unconscious, continue influence the person's behavior and being experienced by him as fears, worrying.

Repression: stage 519617 918421 – two stages: primary and secondary.

Repression secondary 599871319611 – repression

genuinely, concerns psychic derivatives of repressed representation, associated with a drive, or thoughts, originated from other sources but associated with these representations in association.

Repression primary 598712689317 – the 1st phase of repression consists in not permitting
of psychic repression of a drive in consciousness.

Repression sexual 519514819 314 – one of the features of hysterical character, consists in going out of limits of normal resistance against sexual affection increase such as shame, morality and instinctive escape from intellectual studies of sexual problem, in extreme cases coming to the full absence of sexual knowledge just till the achievement of puberty maturity.

_Г_

Hallucination 49871600989 – perceptions, experience at absence of any external stimulation; perception of really absent objects subjectively considered as real. Pathological disturbance of perceptive activity consisting of perception of objects which at the given moment do not influence on the corresponding sensory organs. It usually arises from different psychic disorders in stressed situations and also during the long sensory isolation.

Hedonism 498714898 – antic notion, means joy and pleasure in ancient Greek philosophy of Cyrenaica, it was the ground of the study that admitted delight (pleasure) as the sense of life not only corporal but spiritual.

Hemeralopia 5142842 – deterioration of visual perception in feeble light.

Hemianopsia 519481 319711 – loss of ability to perceive left or right part of visual field. It determined by damage of nervous traits of visual analysers in area of cerebral chiasma or higher. When damaging of inner parts of chiasma the partial blindness appears as external visual field. When damaging of nervous traits of cortical part of visual analysers of one of the cortical hemisphere the partial blindness appears as opposite visual field.

Gene 488713918 913 – discrete structural unity located in a chromosome and responsible for the transfer of congenital features. The number of genes is varied from 50 to 100000 for different types.

Gene major 514891419311 – the gene, which presence provides the display defined by its feature independently weather another gene of the same pair is major or recessive.

Gene recessive 519 016 89 – the gene able to provide the display of the defined feature only when it is not in the pair with corresponding major gene.

Generalization 319891418 – the process when a subject reproduces behavioral reaction responded to all irritants or situations, similar to unconditioned irritant or situation for which the support was made.

Generativity 491814 718314 – an interest to the next generation and its education, revealed productiveness and creativity in various spheres of life of a human, achieved 40 years and who positively experiences a crisis correspondent to this age.

Genetics 219716 818717 – division of biology studied the laws of inheritance of features. Genetics must not be confused with genetic psychology studied the development of behavior from the moment of birth to death.

Genetic behavioral 514312 819 718 216 – division of genetics devoted to the research of regularities of inherited conditions of functional display of the nervous system activity. The main tasks are the description of the mechanisms of gene realization at behavioral features and description of the environment influence on the process.

Genius 519 007 918 788 – the highest level of the development of abilities such as general, intellectual and special. One may speak of its presence only if a personality achieves such results of creative activity which is an epoch in the life of society and culture development; the features are characteristic for genius such as creative productiveness, mastering of a certain methodology, readiness to overcome stereotypes and conventional attitudes.

Genitalia 489791698 – sexual, genitals organs.

Genotype 319681719311 - genetic constitution, complex of genes of the given organism, inherited from parents.

Hermaphrodism 519518619710 – bisexuality i.e. presence of male and female features in one and the same organism.

Hermeneutics 428714317918 – 1. The art, theory, tradition and methods of interpretation of polysemantic texts or texts, not beggaring for elaboration. 2. The art of consideration, comprehension of polysemantic symbols, allegories etc.

Hermeneutics psychoanalytic 548712328 412 – one of the psychoanalytic focused branch of modern philosophy. It researches problems of linguistic communication and processes of socialization, in which, as it supposes, symbols are formed.

Gerontological psychology 494711918991 – the psychology of mature age and oldness (developmental psychology).

Heterogeny 914811718911 – the feature of statistic sampling, the data of which to the essential degree are spread along the scale of distribution, that is expressed by big standard deviation and witnesses of strong difference of the data one from another.

Heterohypnosis 489317619 817 – the hypnosis, produced by influence of another person.

Heterosuggestion 819488719318 – suggestion, an influence from outside. The object of heterosuggestion is either a person or a group, social layer etc. (the phenomenon of mass suggestion); the source of suggestion is an individual, group, means of mass information.

Gestalt 819317918217 8 – a functional structure, according to subsistent laws regularizes the variety of separate phenomena. It means the whole, not reduced to the summary of its parts, the construction of consciousness: seeming movement, insight, perception of a melody etc.

Gestalt-group 498716818 – groups, forming with the aim of psychotherapeutic influence in gestalt therapy.

Gestalt psychology 318714918514 – the branch of psychology put the program of research of psyche from the view point of whole structures i.e. gestalts primary relatively to their components.

Gestalt therapy 514 788 918 312 – In the capacity of the approach to psychological correction it is one of the most influential trend in modern psychology.

Hydrophobia 548712 618317 – a type of neurosis characterized by psychological phobia of water.

Hyperactivity childish 519488 71631 – deviation from age norms of ontogenetic development; characterized by inattention, distractibility, impulsiveness in social behavior and intellectual activity, high activity at normal level of intellectual development. All this leads to weak progress in studies and low self-estimation.

Hypermnesia 591061319 811 – exaggerated usually congenital ability to memorize information (visual, symbolic) in bulk or for a very long time.

Hyperpathia 598715 918065 – increasing of sensitivity, characterized by appearance of pain or other unpleasant senses as response to usually harmless irritants.

Hypoesthesia 598716318917 – increasing of sensitivity to physical stimuli, influencing on an organism; expresses appearance of extremely strong subjective senses without change of their modality.

Hypnoanalysis 598764 988 314 – diagnostic procedure for which the composition of anamnesis or revealing of the content of client's life emotional experiences is carried out when he becomes immersed with hypnosis.

Hypnosis 498 712688001 – 1. The procedure, influence on an individual by concentration of his attention with the aim to narrow the field of consciousness and subdue it to the influence, control of external agent hypnotist, whose suggestions a person immersed with hypnosis will fulfill. 2.

The process and temporal dreamlike state of psyche, characterized by sharp narrowed and taken away conscious and self-consciousness volume and sharp focusing on the content of suggestion, which is associated with the change of the function of individual control and self-consciousness. It appears as the result of special impact of the hypnotist or purposeful suggestion.

Hypnosis ablative 49178909 1069 – hypnotic method, characterized by the fact that a client is put into hypnotic state without actual presence of a hypnotist whose treatment interview is recorded on audio or video cassette. A client can be at home at the moment.

Hypnosis active graded 498716 318719 – hypnotic method based on the conscious control of relaxation.

Hypnopedia 818742 319622 – phenomenon of the information input and fixation in memory during a natural dream, also the method of teaching and educating when dreaming, based on this phenomenon. Especially effective for fixation of homogenous information: foreign words, formulas, Morse alphabet etc. It is marked expressed exhaustion of a testee after the treatment interview of hypnopedia.

Hypnotization 317814219887 18 – stimulation of hypnotic state, performed by a hypnotist or by a subject himself by the way of verbal or nonverbal impact.

Hypnotism 489714 719317 – general definition of complex of phenomena, arising during hypnosis. At times it's the synonym to the notion of hypnosis.

Hypomnesia 489317918 - worsening of memory congenital or acquired as a result of different diseases.

Hypothalamus 918 671 818 971 – the structure of transitional cortex, under thalamus. It contains 12 pairs of nucleus i.e. the most important centers of vegetative functions. More than that, it is tightly associated with hypothesis, which activity it regulates.

Hypothesis 498716 319818 – scientific supposition put for explanation of some phenomena which needed to be practically checked up and theoretically grounded to acquire the status of scientific theory. In terms of psychology it's a supposition of separate features of reality, put for orientation of activity and determined by existing in a person subject picture of the world.

Hypothesis alternative 314817 818 91 – hypothesis according to which the difference among statistic samplings are essential reflects corresponding difference inside the population or among populations where these samplings were taken. Usually it corresponds to the working hypothesis of the researcher.

Hypothesis of memorizing interference 488716 918 917 Explanatory model according to which the process of forgetfulness is caused by the fact that new coming data is put on the already existing one what leading to the destruction of its associative ties.

Hypothesis conceptual propositional 59871639816 – an assumption, formulated as the conception of associative memory towards the fact that not image or verbal reflections of situations, but some interpretations of events, forming as concepts and proposals are preserved in the long-time memory.

Hypothesis scientific 498714318 218 – an assumption put forward as temporal on the base of observations and specified by future experiments.

Hypothesis of linguistic relativity 519817419 – the hypothesis of dependency of perception and thinking from ethnotypical language structures. According to it, the language skills and norm of unconscious define images, world pictures inherent to native speakers. Linguistic constructions and vocabulary links, acting on unconscious level, lead to the creation of typical picture of the world inherent to native speakers and acting as a scheme for catalogue of personal experience.

Hypothesis stereochemical 489171 918 – osmesis depends on the interaction of molecules of smelling substance with the membrane of olfactory cell, dependent either on the forms of molecules or the presence in it the certain functional group. The molecule of olfactory cell comes in excitement state under the influence of vibratory molecule of smelling substance, coming into certain receptor's socket on the membrane of the olfactory cell. In this theory 7 primary odors are distinguished: camphor-like, flower, musk, menthol, ether, spicy, rotten. All other smells are complex and consist of some primary ones.

Hippocampus 214 317 814 218 – the structure of deep layer of temporal lobe of cortex. It looks like sea-horse in section from which the name is originated. It belongs to the limbic system and plays the important role in remembering and reproduction of information.

Acrophobia 594816 009 – kind of neurosis, characterized by pathological fear of heights.

Histogram 594817 319 778 – one of the way of graphic presentation of quality data as square columns adjoined to each other and correspondent to the frequency of each class of data.

Eye: movement 598 617 918 312 – eyes circulation in orbits, performing various functions in visual image construction of visual perception of space. It provides measurement and analysis of space attributes of objects i.e. a form, position, size, distance, velocity of movement. The most important of these movements is the centering of the object image on the retina what provides the highest acuity of visual perception.

Eye: macro-movement 418 713 818 914 – eye movements, performing with the amplitude of more than some tens of angle minutes: vergent and version movements belong to them.

Eye: micro-movement 498 714 818 316 - eye movements with amplitude up to 20-30 at a sight fixation which are not determined by the tasks of recognition. Among them there are: tremor, drift and microsuccades.

Eye: light sensitivity 519 317 818 266 – the ability of an eye to form visual senses responding to electro-magnetic radiance with certain length of waves (from 350 to 750 nm).

Homeostasis 498716 319 816 – mobile equilibrium state of a system, preserving by the way of its contraction to the inner and outer disturbing the balance factors. It is a support of the continuity of various physiological parameters of an organism.

Homeostasis 219317 818 91481 – technical model device supporting a value or complex of values at the necessary level. It imitates homeostasis adaptation of living organisms to the changeable environment.

Homogeneity 514321819311 – the attribute of the statistic sampling, data of which concentrated around an average arithmetic value or median reveals small value of standard deviation and witnesses little difference among data.

Homosexuality 598 016 649081 – the notion defines sexual inclination of a person to representatives of the same gender and sexual relations between them. Male homosexuality is also called pederasty; name for female one is lesbianism.

Homophobia 481 398019 644 – irrational hostility even hatred towards homosexuals. It is often the mean of psychological self-defense from own unconscious homoerotic senses, fancies, motives at the level of individual consciousness.

Hospitalism 498716 3987210 69 – the pathological syndrome of a of child psychic and personal development caused by an isolation of a baby from its mother and its institutionalization. It is to be deep psychic and physical retardation determined by lack of communication with grown-up during the 1^{St} year of child's life. It puts the negative trace on all spheres of forming personality, inhibits intellectual and emotional development, distorts ego-conception, destructs physical wellbeing etc.

Preparedness (readiness) to activity 519384 919284 – attitude, aimed at the performance of an action.

Gradient 548719 814 316 – regular qualitative change reflects worsening or increase of some feature or factor, e.g.

excitation gradient.

Goal gradient 519 006078916 – change of the force of motivation of an activity depending on 'psychological distance' to the aim, typical increasing of motivation and activity in the course of approaching to the desired aim time.

Graphology 548712 818 912 – study of handwriting as a kind of impressive movement variety expressed psychic properties and state of a subject.

Graphomania 319481519 006 – irresistible passion for writing of a person who is deprived of necessary abilities.

Day dream (reverie) 219817 318887 – a fancy, a dream, drawing in one mind's eye pleasant, desired images of future or often illusive 'real' life.

Loudness 498714 319844 – subjective measure of sound intensity perception. Unity of loudness, phon as a measure quantitatively corresponds to the level of sound pressure of a tone 1000 Hz: so, the sound intensity of 20 phon corresponds to the tone of 1000 Hz with intensiveness of 20 db higher than auditory threshold. Subjective volume of a sound is defined not only by signal intensity but its frequency.

Group 451 689319 87 – limited in size people community, distinguishing or distinguished from social entity by certain features: character of activity, social or class position, structure, composition, level of development etc.

Group large 519316 919 817 90 – 1. Not limited in number contingent people community, distinguished basically on the certain social features: class position, gender, age, nationality etc. 2. Actual essentially large organized group, involved in a social activity (staff of an institute, school, office). Standard of behavior, social and cultural values and traditions (social attitudes, mass movement, that are conducted to the consciousness of every person through small groups) are worked out in large groups.

Age group 598716 318711 – one of the types of contingent large group of people attached in the nature of age.

Group encounter 519317 418981 – special small groups applied in the practice of social-psychological training. The aim of the encounter training is to find and use some hidden reserves of personal self-development through special techniques, which help clients to recognize own abilities and to get rid of complexes, psychological barriers.

Group diffusive 819481 919 317 – community in which there is no cohesion as value-oriented unity and there is no common activity able to mediate relations of its members.

Group control 514 517 814319 – group of testee for which results received in research in experimental group are compared on the purpose to receive conclusions weather the checked up hypothesis proved.

Group small 419317819448 – rather small number of individuals contacted directly and united in the nature of common aims and tasks.

Group informal 5914 714819061 – real social community being of no legal fixed status and associated by goodwill on the ground of common interests, friendship, sympathy or pragmatic utility.

Psychodrama group 591489 711 316 – special small groups in which clients recognize better and solve their problems more effectively through role behavior. It is acquired when training roles which allow adapting for life more successfully.

Group actual 598712319 884 – in terms of social psychology limited in number people community existed in common space and time and associated by actual relations e.g. at school class, brigade, military subdivisions, family etc. The less actual group is dyad of two interacting individuals.

Group referential 498716 319007 – group, the aims, opinions and values of which the given person accepts to the more or less degree. Actual or contingent social community to which the individual corresponds himself as to a model and on which standards, opinions, values and estimations he is focused respective his behavior and self-estimation.

Group of body therapy 598716 389764 groups where great importance is given to strait body contacts of clients as the mean of deprivation from psychological problems.

Group of skills training 594817798064 – groups members of which produce useful for life skills that is communicative; due to acquired skills clients may get rid of uncertainty, anxiety, aggressiveness and other forms of negative behavior.

Group contingent 918719069319 – associated by certain features sort of activity, gender, age, level of education nationality etc. people community, including subjects having no direct or indirect objective interrelations with each other. People constituted the community may not only ever meet but do not know each other though they are in certain, more or less equal relations with other members of their actual groups.

Group formal 548700 984317 – actual or contingent social community having legal status, members of which under conditions of socially divided labor are associated by the given activity socially. Formal groups always have normative fixed structure, elected or appointed leaders, normative fixed rights and duties of its members. e.g.: commissions, groups of referents, consultants etc.

Group experimental 518740989 600 – group of testee, the research of which is performed for the purposes to check up some hypothedimensions.

Groupment 528714 308967 – structure of logics. It is considered to be the linking tie between logical and psychological structures.

Grouping 519687918 422 – transformation of the actual active and primarily diffusive human community to the community of interacting and interdependent persons i.e. the group of certain level of development in the course of common activity. The variant of group construction is collective construction i.e. the transformation of the group into collective, when it passed some stages of development, typical not only external changes(time of existence, amount of communications, relation power sub-ordination, quality of sociometric choices etc) but certain phenomena of interpersonal relations (unity, value-oriented, collective self-definition, identification, motivation of interpersonal choices, reference etc.) appearing on the ground of common activity, socially valuable and personally significant for all group members.

Humanism 519888 009 611 – it shows as deep respect to a person and his dignity, an active fight against all forms of human hatred. It includes the knowledge of life, positive attitude to people, their life and activity, human love and soul warmth as a personal feature.

Humanity 519 618 887 998 – attributable to moral standard and values the system of personal attitude to social objects (a man, a group, living beings), showed in consciousness as sense of compassion and realized in communication and activity of collaboration, cooperation, help, etc.

Pressure 897489 712 698 – differs from the need only by its targeting: if the emanated from an organism dynamic force is need, pressure is the force having an effect on an organism.

Daltonism 598671 889 001 98 – inherited anomaly of color vision, expressed as non-sufficient or even complete non-distinguishing of some colors.

Data: statistical processing 598067 998 7102 – what kind of aims and methods of psychological researches may be, the data received as the result might be considered the results of measurement of various psychological phenomena etc. The procedure of quantitative values referring to the researched objects according to certain rules is understood as measuring.

Data primary 598064 018 712 – the information on examined events received at the beginning of the research and entitled to further processing in order to get the possible true conclusions about these phenomena that may be made on its ground.

Movement 688071 981 069 – structural unity of practice as the result of work of psychophysiologic apparatus when realizing of motor act by mean of which the interaction of living being with external environment goes. Psychological activity of an organism shows as movement.

Movement: coordination 510609 499 012 – control of a separate muscles group work, performed when a certain problem solving on real time and space basis.

Movement: organization: mechanism 519765 819355 the object of research are natural movements of normal organism, mainly, human.

Movement: construction 598761 029311 –It is the main notion of the theory of functioning of human motility. Construction of movement is realized at the expense of the work at some levels, each of them originates not the separate qualities of one movement but the whole specter of full value movements.

Movement: psychic regulation 598741 228 011 – (Psychic regulation of movements) the adjustment of construction of movement on the basis of requirement of the state and the feedback that verifies its achievement

Movement vergent 529 161 789 019 –macro movements of eyes leading to a change of the angle between the visual axes of the left and right eye

Movement versive 529061 789071 2 - 1. Macro movements of eyes adding vergent movements. Among them there are:1) fast saccadic through the use of which the correction of eyes position is provided. 2) slow tracking movements by which the adjusted rate of eye movements towards the objectives are at constant distance from the observer, and 3) the compensatory eye movement (vestibular origin) ensure preservation of the visual axis direction by changing the position and speed of the head movement

Movement expressive 298061789011 –outward expression of mental states especially emotional, expression of emotional experiences and intentions of the individual. Manifested in facial expressions (movements of the facial muscles of expression: expression, smile, eye movement), pantomime (expressive movements of the body, body movement, posture, gestures) and "vocal mimicry" that is, the dynamic aspects of speech (intonation, pitch, vibrato voice). Expressive movements are often accompanied by changes in heart rate, respiration, endocrine glands, etc.

Movement: life: heterogeneity 598716 018 914 – functional structural and morphological complexity of motorial act. Each component of movement (cognitive, program, affective, estimating) may vary under real conditions of motorial behavior in response to the change of motorial task, situation, inner recourses of movements and functional states of an individual.

Movement seeming 897128 89812129 – an illusion, characterized by subjective perception of motion in consequent presentation of nonmotile stimuli placed in different parts of space. It may show as visual system, auditory or tactile. Cinematograph was grounded by using of the illusion.

Movement involuntary 948 049 817 217 – impulsive or reflective motorial action, producing out of conscious control. It may be adaptive in nature as winking; withdrawal hands when exposed to painful stimulus, or non-adaptive, as chaotic motions in situation of stupefaction.

Movement post arbitrary 489 716 318 717 –formed as voluntary movements, but after the subsequent deactivation of the orienting basis during their formation they are derived from consciousness, become automated and involuntary movements. They can again be made arbitrarily without special formation work

Movement voluntary 8898 891 319 189 – inner and outer body motorial action, consciously regulated by a subject based on the need to achieve goals as a way of anticipating of the outcome. They suppose conscious orientation in relation to the goal, either in terms speech or in terms of imagination.

It may be performed through skeleton muscles, realizing space body movements and smooth muscles of inner organs (blood vessels), realizing vegetative functions.

Movement voluntary: formation 988 319 817 89908 – transfer of management to conscious control in construction of motions.

De-automation 899019 23 517 – loss of ability to perform motorial skills, earlier automated, without actual conscious control. It may be caused by influence of external impacts or by occurring in time of natural forgetting of the elements of the skill. It also may witness neuropsychological changes in damages of pre-motorial lobe of cerebrum.

Mental debility (moronity) 8980 719 88 091 – mild degree of mental retardation.

Deduction 519712 819 06489 – movement of knowledge from more general to less general, partial; inference from premises. It is tightly associated with induction. Logic considers deduction as a type of thought conclusion. Psychology researches development and violation of deductive reasoning. Movement of knowledge from the more general to the less general is analyzed as one conditioned by all mental processes, the structure of mental activity in general

Action 598712 684367 – voluntary intentional mediate activity, aimed at achievement of conscious goal.

Action and operation 598712 684367 88 - Any complex action consists of the layer of actions and the layer of subordinate to them operations. The boundary of layers of acts and operations is mobile; its movement upward means transformation of some acts, elementary mainly, into operations: extension of unities of activity occurs. Movement of a boundary downward means transformation of operations into actions; subdivision of activity into smaller unities occurs.

Action: orientating basis 9 58712 68436 491 – system of representation of an aim, plan and means of fulfillment of further (next) or carried out action.

Action: motorial composition 712 684367 4719 811 – is the system of motorial operations, making in correspondence to the motorial task, the finish of its construction is possible only in the process of practical work, leading to the amplification of individual style of movements.

Action automatic (primary) 519489 68 998 – this group consists of congenital act or those, that is formed very early, often during the 1st year of child's life. They are: sucking movements, winking, grasping, eyes convergence and others. Automatic actions are unconscious and often trials to recognize them usually damage these actions.

Action voluntary 591814 391882 – it is associated with recognition of an aim of action or, at least, their nearest possible results.

Action impulsive 5498713916 7809 – it appears suddenly for a person; provoked by emotions and realizing of their consequences comes only after completed action. Here is the more ancient and fast way of reaction work.

Action instrumental 684367 – an action serving as a mean of achievement of an aim, different from the result of the action.

Action executive 598712 8679101 – formed skill of assigned speed and accuracy in the construction of which the certain set of industrial operations and corresponding instruments of work are used: instruments, control-measuring devices, organs of control etc.

Repetition compulsion 59881919 711 – involuntary symptomatic and psychological actions, producing, in spite of desire and often in spite of restraining efforts. In most cases they act as mediator, providing the satisfaction of banned unconscious desire and getting of release.

Action erroneous (faulty) 519 080 598 2188901 – general name for whole class of actions with 'defects', faults of different nature in their performance are found out. They are: slip of the tongue, slip of the pen, mishearing, forgetting, loss, memory mistakes and mistakes of aberration i.e. the manifestation of a fight of two opposite unconscious strivings (intentions and resistivity), as the result of which the intended action is damaged and the fault action comes about.

Action perceptive 914 8901 4819 – main structural unities of the process of perception. It provides conscious detachment of an aspect of sense stimulated situation, and also transformation of sensory information, leading to image construction, adequate to the objective world and task of activity.

Action perceptive vicarious 419316 819 013 98 – perceptive acts of visual system. Directed to the analysis of information, that is a trace from stimulation of retina receptors; performed through low amplitude eyes motions (drift, fast leaps) leading to selective changes of sensitivity of separate parts of retina. They are subjectively realized as the displacement of attention in the limits of stabilizing visual image.

Action instrumental (objective) 891316719 891 – more complex psychological formation than proper actions. Directly associated with the aim of activity; has certain objective content. Formed objective actions, become personal property, act as skills – the methods of behavior and activity.

Action symptomatic 594 892 007 314 – actions, seemed to be occasional, aimless (singing melodies to oneself, handling things etc.).

Action accidental 891016 319078 – various, unnoticed and insignificant excessive actions, seeming like occasional, but actually they are psychic acts in full and the signs of other, more important spiritual processes at the same time.

Action mental 519 317989411 - system of intellectual operations, aimed at founding out of object's features, not given in perceptive terms from mathematic transformation to estimation of other human behavior, performed in inner context of consciousness, without support of external means included speech.

Deuteranopia 919716 319817 – disorder of perception of separate colors, mostly green specter, usually caused by inborn factors. Light-green does not differ from dark-red, violet from blue, purple from grey. The point of highest perceptible lightness is shifted to the side of red specter and placed in its orange part; neutral point corresponds to the wave length of 500Hm.

Delinquent 519 671 3190841 – a subject, whose behavior is deviant in extreme manifestations and is criminally punishable action.

Delirium 519481719 379 – damage of consciousness, distorted reflection of reality; accompanied by hallucination, delirium, motor excitement, violation of orientation in time and space. It may alternate with periods of bright consciousness and critical attitude to painful manifestations. It often appears to the uttermost of some inflective diseases, after traumas, caused organic damages of brain.

Dementia 591899016791 89 – acquired from mental debility as the result of not sufficient development or atrophy of highest psychic functions. Associated with reduction of intellectual abilities, emotional poverty, difficulties in use of former experience.

Boxer's dementia 548 791398761 5118 – the term, means clinic state of boxers, characterized by process of increase of mental debility as the result of strokes on the head. Starts with mild psychic and psychological disorder and then comes to sharply expressed characterological and psychomotor defects.

Depersonification 319 488 891728 -1. Change of individual self-consciousness, typical for which are loss of psychological and behavioral peculiarities, characteristic for his personality, senses of loss of own ego and painful experience of absence of emotional involvement in relations with relatives, work etc. It is possible for mental diseases and in-between state. It is observed for psychic healthy people when emotionally overloaded and suffering from somatic diseases etc. in mild form. 2. Expressed as more or less degree objective loss by an individual of the possibility to be ideally represented in life activity of other people, to find out the ability to be a personality.

Depression 519514 319891 – in terms of psychology affective state, characterized by negative emotional background, changes in motivational sphere, cognitive presentation and general passive behavior. Subjectively a person experiences first of all heavy painful emotions and experiences i.e. suppression, despair, melancholia. Drives, motives, volitional activity are sharply decreased.

Deprivation sensory (input) 891671 319 064 – long, more or less full deprivation of sensory impressions for a man, realized at experimental aims.

Derialization 489719 016891 – damage of perception, where the external world is perceived as unreal or distant, deprived of its colors, and damages of memory take place. It is often accompanied by the state of already seen or never seen. May occur in damages of brain (deep lobe of temporal areas), in states of awakeness, psychic diseases.

Dereflection 5193718 919890619 – psychotherapeutic technique, that consists in the fact that a client, suffering from some functional symptoms, formulates the aim for himself: 1) submit to it, perceiving as irresistible evil; 2) in the situation which provokes its display to turn his attention from the damaged function to another activity, so attaching of other sense to the situation. Due to it the situation is not already considered as one more attempt to get rid of the symptom, but as the possibility of full value communication with people.

Dermatoglifics 917 31861988 89 – recently appeared new branch of knowledge studies the development of finger lines in correspondence with heredity.

Destructiveness 419 688 789 0179481 – the ground of the most malignant destructiveness and non-humanism and also heavy pathological state is the syndrome of disintegration.

Destruction 589761669 31 – destruction, damage of normal structure of something, elimination.

Detector 489 37188997691 – a device for finding out of

certain type of signals. They are the components of analysers.

Determination 559 3178890619 – causal conditioning of phenomena and processes.

Determinism 598061890619 89 – conception, according to which people's actions are determined or defined and limited by inherent and previous life events. In terms of psychology it is regular and essential dependence of psychic phenomena on the factors they are originating from.

Determination dual 598 761319841 – intentions and fancies; approval by consciousness conclusions of such actions, in motivation of which displaced took part.

Children: age development 59148901739 8 – one can separate a set of age periods: baby age, early age, preschool, school junior, teenage, youth early.

Children; MOTOR DEVELOPMENT 591 489 016 7 – the process of qualitative change of child system of movement during his growth and collecting of individual experience. The main set of universal motorial reactions is finally formed up to 11-14 years.

Children affective 591 068 398716 – children, having constant negative emotional experience and destructive behavior, caused by unsatisfied needs important for him. The forms of destructive behavior are different. One child in situation of failure does not accept it, what may be displayed as brave, arrogant, aggressive behavior. For others typical is decrease of demands' level accompanied by uncertainty, fear of disappointment, offensiveness, sensitiveness. When constantly reproduced inadequate responses to failure acquire the form of constant features of character.

Children gifted 489761 398063 - children have general or special gifts – for music, drawing, technique etc. Children's gifts is diagnosed by the tempo of mental development that is the level of advance under other equal conditions of juniors of the same age the test of mental gifts and coefficient of intellect are based on that.

Childhood 489067 319227 – the term means initial period of ontogenesis from birth to teen age (in wide sense till the appearing of ability to be involved in adult life).

Defectology 598 063714 0 – science researches regularities and features of children development with physical and psychic disorders, and also the tasks of their education and teaching.

Decentration 51906421 9712 – mechanism of the overcoming of a personal egocentrism, consisting in the change of subject's position as the result of clash, comparison and integration with positions, different from his own.

Act 891719 014 314 – the form of manifestation of subject's activity, defined by its socially significant results, the responsibility for which the subject takes even if they come out of limits of his intentions. Personal responsibility of the subject's action is defined on the ground of concrete social-historical criteria of estimation of his potentialities to anticipate the results of his activity. Action is a particular form of unity of psychological and sociological description of subject's activity and it can be used as the unity of psychological analysis of personality. Personalization of the individual for the system of interpersonal relations is provided through actions.

Activity 598741 998 241 – dynamic system of active interactions of a subject with external world, when the subject purposefully influences on an object, and so, satisfies his needs; appearance and embodiment of psychic image in the object occurs and realization of mediate by it the relations of the subject in objective reality.

Activity and communication 518741228231 – in the process of activity the relations kind of subject-object are opened that is the objective world of human being, and in the process of communication there do relations kind of subject-object as interpersonal relations of people, person's relation to society. In terms of social psychology there is a postulate on the unity of communication and activity on one hand, communication is considered as the side of activity; on the other hand activity and communication are two sides of human being and way of life.

© Grabovoi G.P., 2003

Activity: individual style 598041788 918 – constant individual specific system of psychological means, techniques, skills, methods of performance of some activity.

Activity: structure 598714 318 – (macrostructure) – from the position of structure there are movements and actions in activity.

Activity leading 548769 018 998 – from the position of active approach to the research of psychics it is the activity with which the appearance of the most important new psychic formations is bound at the given stage of development, in course of the process other types of activity are developed and the grounds for transition to new leading activity is founded.

Activity inner 519 891 419 31891 – any mental work not obligatory mental process itself, but mental reproduction of next actions, planning. It has very important function: inner actions prepare external actions and minimize efforts for choice of necessary actions. Also allow to avoid rude and crucial faults.

Activity childish 488719 816 098 – active interaction of a child with external world, when ontogenetic construction of its psyche occurs.

Activity cooperative (collective) 519317 914899 – concerning social-psychological aspect it is variant of joint activity, based on group possession of means of production and also final product of work.

Activity of an operator 599061 899072 – control of technical devices, immediately influence on the object of activity instead of a man.

Activity tentative 598761 019311 – behavior, based on research of environment objects with the aim to form an image of the space, where the object's activity must be performed; complex of subject's actions, aimed at active orientation in situation , investigation and planning of behavior.

Activity special 517 488091499 – complex of actions, called by one motive.

Action objective 981814319 01 – activity, subordinated the peculiarities of objects of material and spiritual culture; practical actions with real objects of material and spiritual culture, according to their functional and culturally determined purpose. Aimed at acquire of ways of correct use of these objects and at development of abilities, skills.

Activity mental 598 061719081 – psychological analysis allow to classify it from the position of functions, performed in the process of interaction of a man with world and other people. Here one can say about tentative, executive functions and function of comparison and control.

Activity mental: determination 519617 019488 89 - classic formula of psychoanalysis: in psychic there is no arbitrariness at all.

Activity rational 519171 819 311 – its display is noted in primitive animals and then it increases sharply at the level of highest primates and achieves maximum with human.

Activity over (super normative) 518 141988 051 – goodwill, out of limits of established social norms, the activity of a subject or a group, directed to help of other people.

Activity of dream 5480668 917 398 – the process of transfer of hidden content of a dream into real so is one of the whole row of similar psychic processes, causing also the origin of hysteroid symptoms, obsessive ideas, fancy and pathological phobias.

Activity joint 514 966963 019 – in terms of social psychology it is organized system of activity of interacting individuals, directed towards the purposeful production, reproduction of objects of material and spiritual culture.

Activity working 514518 19898 – it plays important role in human life independent from the form of performance of activity. It is on what namely the existence of a man and society depends.

Activity learning 514 889 0167891 – leading activity of school primary age where the foundations of social and cognitive experience occur, first of all as main intellectual (mental) operations and theoretical notions.

Diagnosis 519006 319789 – definition of a disease root and state of a patient on the ground of his complete medical observation.

Diagnosis psychological 588016 079 891 23 – the main aim of psychodiagnostics; the eventual result of psychologist's activity aimed at description and clearing out of the essence of an individual psychological peculiarities of personality on the purposes of estimation of their actual state, prognosis of further development and making out of recommendation, that is defined by the matter of observation. The subject of psychological diagnosis is establishment of individual psychological features either towards standard or pathology.

Diagnostics 598 561988079 – the division of medicine studying signs of a disease, methods of research of patients and principles of establishment of diagnosis.

Diagnostics psychological 599061718918 971 – psychodiagnostics dialogue as talk exchange of two or more people. In wide sense a retort it is also the response as an action, gesture, silence. Each reply of a dialogue as the unite of individual speech has objective correspondence and social nature (turned to a partner, regulated by micro social relations between partners). Dialogue being ontogenetically previous to inner speech makes an impact on its structure and functions and thus on consciousness in whole.

Scope, range (range of variations) 589061 318 – difference between max and min values in the frames of the given range.

Didactogenia 598716 389718 – determined by disorder of pedagogic tact from a teacher's side, trainer etc. the specific state of a pupil (suppressed mood, fear), negatively reflected in his activity and interpersonal relations. It may be the reason of neurosis.

Dynamic group 891 488 311489 – complex of in-group social-psychological processes and phenomena, characterizing the whole cycle of life activity of a little group and its stages, education, formation, function, development, stagnation, regress, disintegration.

Diplopia 5948 581619 7198 – phenomenon of dual vision of an image in declination to the side of direction of visual axis of one of eyes: the image from one eye coincides with an object, but the image from other eye(with declined axis) goes out of object's limits and disposes close. After correction of visual axis of an eye the image correlates with the object again.

Dippoldizm 418716388 917 – special type of sadism, when a subject achieves his sexual satisfaction in torture of his pupils.

Dysgraphia 598718 419 399 – disorder of writing, accompanied by letter substitution, gaps, letter and word alternation, cohesion of words. It is caused by damage of speech system in whole; considered as the symptom of alalia, in various forms of aphasia in lack of speech development.

Discrimination 518417 398678 – ability distinctly perceives two similar stimuli, simultaneously influence on two close placed parts of skin. In wide sense it is differentiation; the ability to differentiate.

Discrimination intergroup 591489 019681 – establishment of differences between own and other group.

Dysmorphophobia 801 061 988 – a kind of neurosis, characterized by pathological phobia to look like a freak.

Dispersion (variance) 591848 17019 – the mark of dispersion of data, corresponding to the quadrate of declination of the data from arithmetic mean. It is equal to the square of standard deflection.

Disposition (predisposition) 591 619 081 9 – readiness or predisposition of a subject to behavioral act, actions or their consequence. In personal psychology terms it means causal not conditional inclination to actions. For purposes of home psychology the term is used mainly for the definition of conscious preparedness of a person to estimate situation and behavior, determined his previous experience.

Dissimulation 519 068719 331 – behavior opposite

to the simulation which associated with the attitude to hide, to shade a disease, its symptoms or separate manifestations.

Dissonance 518411 718906 – absence of harmony in something; non-correspondence, discord.

Dissonance cognitive 598061318 719 – contradiction in the system of knowledge, originated in a subject's unpleasant experiences and stimulating for action, directed to the removal of this contradiction.

Dissociation 899061 718917 – in terms of psychology violation of cohesion of psychic processes. The opposite notion is association.

Dissociation hysterical 519488 719317 – phenomena of distractibility in case of hysteria.

Distress 598761489891- negative influence of stresses and stress situations on activity up to its complete destruction.

Dysphoria 5987610 8912 – decreased mood with irrelativeness, offensiveness, dull, high sensitivity to the actions of other people, inclination for aggression splashes. Sometimes it may be expressed apathetic, as elevated or exulted mood with aggressiveness, tension. Especially it is typical at organic brain disorders, epilepsy, also in some forms of psychopathia (explosive, epileptic).

Dysfunction 511 019489 48 – violation, disorder of the functions of an organ, system etc. mainly of qualitative nature.

Dysfunction cerebral (minimal) – 918415 9189016 – mild disorders of behavior and education without bright mental disorders, appearing from the lack of functions of the central nervous system; more often has residential-organic nature.

Differentiation 59806 18719 41 – as in-group process the position, status of members of the given community (a group, society etc.). Each member has certain position from the position of authority, occupied position. To display of individual status in a group some sociometric methods are used.

Differentiation sexual 514312 848741 – complex of genetic, morphological and physiological attributes, on the ground of which male and female gender are differentiated. It is fundamental and universal feature of living, associated with the function of reproduction. It is determined as social-cultural for a man. From the moment of definition of passport gender of a newborn the process of his gender socialization begins to transfer to him the form of social behavior corresponding to sexual role.

Differentiation 598612781319 - 1. The process by which an individual does not respond to the options of the stimulus, after which the stimuli are not made unconditional or reinforcing agents, and reproduces the behavioral responses only to those stimuli, which continue to be supported. 2. Exact process of distinction, distinguishing certain stimuli or objects of a different kind, identifying differences between some of them from others.

Dogma 519 4887193178 – an element of some doctrine or religion, considered as absolute truth, indisputable, beyond doubts.

Dominant 548 717519 488 – temporally governing reflector system, some area of psychological stimulation of the central nervous system, where the switching of irritants occur, usually indifferent to this area. It causes the work of new centers at the given moment and so attaches certain direction to behavior.

Donjuanizm 598061 718914 – psychotic state of a man, his typical striving for constant change of a partner and inability to see in a man-woman relation nothing except a body, sexual aspect.

Credibility 519488 718917 – one of the characteristics of psychodiagnostic methods and tests. The notion of credibility is close to the notion of validity, but not analogue.

Drive 8914897163 14 – the notion used in motivational psychology and in the theory of learning. It means unconscious inner drive of general nature, organized by some organic need.

Dramatization 591489 061712 – the process and mechanism of embodiment of thoughts into visual images.

Significant other 589061 098714 – a person important for the given subject of communication and activity. Existing definitions of personal significance falls into 2 main paradigms. The 1st describes significance of other person through changes made by him in the given individual. The 2nd is oriented to correspondence and certain coincidence of other significant features and axiological necessetive sphere of an individual.

Friendship 8901 678 914 81 – kind of stability, individual selective interpersonal relations, characterized by mutual attachment of participants, increase of process of affiliation, mutual expectations of reciprocal feelings and preference. Development of friendship supposes the following unwritten 'codex'. It is asserting the necessity of mutual understanding, openness, belief, active mutual help, interest for affairs and senses of the other, sincerity of senses.

Dualism 8980 17 489417 – 1. Concept affirms the existence of two equal origins. 2. In terms of psychology dualistic approach.

Arc reflex: scheme 519 488 916317 – the principle of arc reflex is spirituality from the naturalistic viewpoint it is individual expression in the system of personal motives of two fundamental needs:1.ideal need of cognition; 2. social need to live and act for others.

Soul (anima) 598061 291319 88 – notion, reflects historically changed views on man's and animal's psyche; in religion, idealistic philosophy and psychology it is soul i.e. life-creating and cognitive origin.

Cordiality 591488 617381 – from materialistic viewpoint individual expression in the system of personal motives of the fundamental social need to live and act for others. This notion is associated with the notion of spirituality. Cordiality is typical kind of relation of a person to surrounding people, attention and readiness to help to participate for joy and grief.

_E_

E-wave (wave of expectation) 519481 068712 – negative change of electric potential mainly in central lobes of brain, associated with tuning to appearance of a stimulus. It appears as time between the action of tuning signal and start signal, that requires some reaction of a testee. Witnesses about readiness to act in perception of a signal. E-wave appears as 0,5 sec after the action of tuning signal. Its amplitude is directly associated with the speed of needed motorial reaction, and also, with tension of attention and will. It allows to consider it as the manifestation of the action of mechanism of voluntary behavior.

Unity 598761 098511 – 1. Unity, complete similarity. 2. Cohesion, wholeness. 3.Mutual tie, inseparability.

Unity dual 589062 488971 – notion for the definition of excessively close neurotic contact, appearing in some love pairs and based on the regress of emotional sphere to the experiences, that have been formed in early childhood in relation to own mother.

Unity axiological orientational 89648 916598721 – one of the basic mark of group cohesion, fixing the degree of coincidence of positions and estimations of its members in relation to aims of activity and values, especially significant for the group in whole. The mark of unity is the frequency of coincidence of positions of group members in relation to object of estimation, significant for them. High degree of value – orientation unity is the important source of intensification of communication in group and increase of efficacy of joint activity.

_Ж_

Blood lust 989061 668436166 – archaic sense and a kind of violence, directed to the self-assertion in the way of bloodshed and murders.

Desire 538417 988069 – conscious drive, reflecting a need; experience coming into active thought of ability to posses something or to perform something.

Desire impulsive 591814918791 068 – in terms of psychoanalysis inherit, involuntary desire of incest, cannibalism, blood lust, desire to kill.

Desirability (advisability) social 598 061918712 – factor, distorting self-concept and responses to the points of personal questioning in the way of increasing of frequency of this self-concept towards that seems more attractive, socially accepted, representing them in profitable light.

Gesture 511 489317499 – an element of pantomime, performed by actions with hands.

Animal: construction activity 599068 909 719 – manipulation with objects; as the result an animal builds complex objects: nests of fish, frogs and birds; various houses of rodents; huts of beavers etc.

Animal: instrumental activity 599061 298 013 – specific form of manipulation with objects, when the action by a separate object is produced by an instrument with another object or animal; behavior, when some objects are used to influence on other objects.

Animal: psychic activity 598748 319891 – whole complex of animal's actions of behavior and animal psyche, directed to the establishment of life necessary ties of an organism with environment; process of reflection of psychic reality as a product and manifestation of animal's activity in external world. It is researched in zoo psychology.

Animal: intellect 548916 319 884 – highest form of mental activity of animals (highest spinal), differs by reflection of not only objective components of environment but their relations and ties (situations), and also by not stereotypic solving of complex tasks – in different way with transition and use of various operations, acquired in previous individual experience.

Animal: thinking 599 891 048916 – process of mental reflection of external world, inherent to highest spinal animals. *It is* characterized by ability of active perception and establishment of ties between objects on the base of general mental images. It realizes by motor-sensorial analysis, directed to the revealing of common features of different situations and formation of utterly generalized image of the sphere of habitual, similar to person's image of the world.

Animal: training 388 916890819 – acquiring and accumulation in ontogenesis of individual experience by animals; improvement and change of inherent (instinctive) base of psychic activity correspondent to concrete conditions of environment. It is readiness for transfer of an individual experience from one, previous situation to new at the expense of which the individual adaptation of living organism to the sphere of living is reached.

Animal: communication 598061 984718 – transfer of information from one creature to other called 'animal language'. Animal communication, in difference from a human's, closed inherent system of signals (sounds, expressive poses, smiles, body motions). The communication through poses, motions may have the form of a ritual.

Animal: behavior 598594 398714 – inherent to creatures the interaction with environment, mediate by their outer (motorial) and inner (psychic) activity, external display of mental activity.

Animal: aggressive behavior 219 006 918782 – threat and actions addressed at representatives of the same or seldom at another type of animals; behavior addressed to its elimination or displacement from sphere of influence.

Animals: group behavior 548 613 988 0491 - coordinated and cooperative action, the behavior of animals (many superior invertebrates and vertebrates) performed during life in the communities, permanent or temporary associations which unlike the clusters have a simple structure of the interactions and communication: herds, flocks, families etc.

Animal: demonstrative behavior 51948191889 818 – form of animal's communication called upon to inform other members about psychological state of an animal. It is often seen in threatening and courtship.

Animal: instinctive behavior 819 061 318941 - complex of formed in the way of development of the given type of animals in terms of phylogenesis inherent fixed, congenital, common for all members of a type, the component of behavior, consisting the base of life activity of animals.

Animal: researching behavior 591897388716 - component of psychic activity, providing biological adequate orientation of their behavior in new situation.

Animal: ritual behavior 598061 789 671 – communication through language of poses and motions, accepting the form of a ritual. Animal's rituals complex set of instinctive actions, lost their primary function and come into other sphere of life activity as signals or symbols.

Animal: territorial behavior 591488 789319 – complex of various forms of animal's activity, aimed at seizure and use of a certain space, with which the performance of these or another life functions is bound (dream and rest, nutrition, reproduction).

Animal: imitation 5980674 819 – special form of learning under conditions of communication, when an animal follows the example of other one.

Animal: psyche: feature 48891678 9061 – differences of animal's psyche from man's psyche. It is usually considered that the base of all forms of animal's behavior, instincts, instinctive actions are genetically fixed, inherent elements of behavior.

Animal: social range (status) 599 061891 67 – forms of social animal's interactions, forming the imitation of hierarchy in their communities.

Animal: community 891641898 712 – life in herds, flacks, families is widely spread among animals. Animal living in communities have complex forms of communication. Typical feature of many communities is the hierarchy of their members.

Life (vital) activity 498716988 079 – complex of types of activity joint by the notion of life and typical for living creatures.

Life 889041 3189888 -1. Complex of phenomena, taking place in an organism. From materialistic view special form of existence and movement of matter, voluntary appeared on the certain stage of its evolution. 2. Physiological existence of living organisms. 3. Subject's activity or community in some manifestations.

Life: aim 598 041 81939178 – achievement of freedom, independence, wholeness and ability to love.

Life: spiritual: polarity 214 2489891 889 – 3 polarities of spiritual life, oppositions, consisting in such relations: 1) subject, Ego-object, outer world; 2) pleasure, satisfaction-non-satisfaction; 3) activeness-passiveness, posses the spiritual life.

Life sexual 591891 068 988 – complex of somatic, psychic, social processes that are moved by sexual drive and through which it is satisfied.

Life sexual normal 591488 798061 – premise and condition corresponding to transformation of sexual drive in the course of the period, when the transformation of infantile sexuality in mature forms occurs.

Life: mental: principle 519512 819389 – fundamental determiner and regulator of activity and psyche of a personality. There are asserted 3 not equal principles: pleasure, reality and stability.

_3_

Disease narcissistic 519 448 7190981 – a disease, determined by pathogenic state of libido, aimed at own ego. Here there are – paraphrenia and paranoia.

Disease neurotic 59874251 898016 – mental disorder; occurs from the conflict between 2 drives: sexual need and deprivation and ousting.

Disease neurotic 519481 71931791 – (essence and tendency of neurotic diseases) – people are ill, if cannot really satisfy erotic need because of outer circumstances or inner lack of adaptability.

Mental illness 8345444 – disease, characterized by

mental disorders mainly.

Psychosomatic illness 819488 7193881 – (psychosomatosis) – the division in medical psychology researches the influence of psychological factors on the appearance of a set of somatic diseases.

Forgetting 428 612 788910 – active process, characterized by step by step decrease of ability to remember and reproduce the learned material, loss of access to previously remembered material; inability to reproduce or to know that was acquired.

Dependence 898716 068 714 – drug dependence or drug addiction. It can be physiological, if an organism itself needs in the given substance for normal (habitual) functioning, or psychological, if this need of affective nature.

Envy 489714318 591 – manifestation of motivation of achievement, when whoever real or illusive advantages in acquiring of social benefits, material goods, success, status, personal qualities etc. are perceived by a subject as a threat to the value of Ego and accompanied by affective senses and actions.

Task closed 5151981489 49 – they are tasks, problems and questions, where an response must be chosen from some given variants.

Task non-verbal 598048 319881 – a task, based exclusively on observation, reasoning and manipulation.

Task imaginative 519 491818918 – contains exercises with images – pictures, drawings, schemes etc. – supposing active use of imagination and mental transformation into images.

Task open 598411 71891817 – they are tasks, problems and questions, where a testee gives an answer by himself.

Task practical 319488 715988 – contains exercises and tasks, which a testee must do visual active that is practically manipulating with real objects or substituents.

Task theoretical 514 817989716 – contains tasks and exercises, which solving requires the display of ability of theoretical thinking. In this sense they are partially close to verbal test tasks as well considering notions, but suppose the application of mental operations of a higher level of abstraction.

Task test 519411899716 – contains exercises and tasks that a testee solves in performing of a test. According to the results the estimations of tested qualities of the testee are given. Many assignments are of complex nature included practical, verbal, theoretical and imaginative actions.

Task test: limited in time 489671 298617 – the demand, according to which the full time of test performance must not be more than 1,5 hours, because it is difficult for a testee to keep high attention for longer period.

Inclination 598 716 388 968 - natural premise of ability; inborn peculiarities of nervous system and brain, consisting in the natural ground for development of abilities.

Task 598716391 898 – an aim of activity, given in certaunder conditions, that may be achieved by transformation of these conditions corresponding to the certain procedure. Task contains objectives (aims), conditions (known) and searched (unknown), formulated in a question. Between these elements certain ties and dependence exist, due to which the search and definition of unknown elements is produced through the already known.

Task: solving 918487 319 444 – in dependence on a style of a person mental activity and accessibility of task content for him, its solving is performed by different ways: 1. method of trials and faults – less typical and less desirable: as a rule it does not lead to accumulation of experience and does not serve the mental development; 2. passive use of algorithm 3. purposeful transformation of conditional task 4. active use of algorithm 5. heuristic ways of solving.

Task motorial 489 44 12 89714 – mental image of movement, that needs its solving, in it there is the information of an aim of movement, of means and ways of task solving.

Retardation 519317 898 711 – inhibition or a stop of

© Grabovoi G.P., 2003

development of some drive or process.

Stammering 898071 318 42 – violation of oral speech, when it becomes breakable, involuntary division of a word into sounds, syllables occurs, convulsive tension of face muscles appear that leads to difficulties in communication with other people.

Law scientific 48712 518 44 – the body of a science are the laws, found constant interties of phenomena, reveal of which allow to describe, explain and foresee phenomena of reality.

Law biogenetic 519 489719 061 – in terms of psychology transfer of correlation between ontogenesis and phylogenesis on the development of child's psyche. Theoretical model, according to which in individual (embryonic) development of highest organisms the regular repetition (recapitulation) of features, inherent their biological forbears.

Bloch law 398417 899 011 – consists in that the value of subjective brightness of sharp flash of light depends on product of intensiveness of light impulse on its duration. But this law acts only in near threshold area and if duration of stimulus does not achieve some critical point.

Weber's law 595 718481319 – one of the main laws of psychophysics.

Weber-Fechner's law 591488 718841 – logarithmic dependence of force of sense E on physical intensiveness of irritant P: $E = k\log P + c$, where k and c – some constants, defined by the given sensory system.

Donders' law 8981 8781891008 – the law of summativeness of psychic (cognitive) process, based on the statement of additivity of its separate parts. On the materials of researches of time of reaction as a process, occurring in the period between appearance of stimuli and realization of backward reaction, Donders grounded the method of subtraction called upon to provide the ability to define the duration of separate stages.

Yerkes-Dodson laws 891619 719884 – establishment

of dependence of quality (productivity) of performed activity at the level of motivation.

Jost law 519481 719 992 – empiric regularity, according to which in equal possibility of reproduction from memory of senseless information, the older information is forgotten slower and requires in learning less number of repetition. On the base of this regularity there is a mechanism of transfer of information from short-time to long-time memory.

Muller-Heckel's law 489161714 312 – biogenetic law- Piper's law– empiric regularity, where the threshold of visual perception decreases proportionally to square root from the area of influence of stimulus under condition that this square is more than 1.

Ribbot's law 489 161 917 891 - regularity, for which in case of progressive amnesia, (in cases of a disease or at an adult age) memory damages have certain sequence. At first, memories of recent events become un-accessible, then subject's mental activity begins to be destroyed; loss of habits and senses; at last, instinctive memory is disintegrated. In case of memory reconstruction the same stages occur in backward order.

Ricco's law 489 716 319 811 – regularity, characterized by the fact that such features of threshold irritant as brightness and angle area of influence are in backward proportional dependence. This law is active for light irritants of small angle dimensions. As its mechanism the nervous summation of irritants is considered, due to which eyes tuning to the perception of light of small intensity occurs.

Stevens' power law 489161719 881 – formula is modification of basic psychophysical law which bounds the strength of sense with certain degree of physical intensiveness of irritants. As to it, between a set of senses and a set of irritants there is no logarithmic correlation, but the power low dependence: $nY=kS$ where Y is subjective value, S is stimuli, n is exponent of power of function, k is constant, depending on the unit of measures. Other writing form: n E=kP where E is strength of senses, P is physical intensity of irritant, k and n are some constants. At that the exponent of power of function for different senses modalities is different: for loudness it is 0,3; for electric shock it is to be 3,5.

Talbot's law 519 377891481 – regularity, according to which visible brightness of the source of breakable light when attaining of glimpses radiance frequency becomes equal to the brightness of constant light with the same values of light flux.

Fechner's law 531489 069718 – the law according to which the value of senses is directly proportional to the logarithm of intensiveness of irritants that is for increase of irritants exponential corresponds to arithmetic progression of the sense's growth. Fechner's postulate was inserted towards the fact that lightly tangible growth of sense is the constant value and it can be used as the unit of sense measurement.

Hick's law 598741 918811 asserts that the time of reaction when choosing from some number of alternative signals depends on their quantity. This regularity acquired the type of logarithmic function: BP=a*log(n+1), where BP is average value of time of reaction on all alternative signals, n is number of equally possible alternative signals, a is coefficient of proportionality. The unit was introduced into the formula to control one more alternative as the gap (loss) of a signal.

Abney's law 491814 31871298 – effect of brightness of some spectral colors when their combining caused the perception of new joint color.

Emmert's law 599 068 718 213 – regularity, according to which the visible value of after-image directly depends on the distance from a screen on which the image is projected. On the ground of the law there is the mechanism providing constancy of visible dimensions of really perceived object. The regularity may not be revealed at large distances from the screen (over 10-15m) and also at eidetic imagery.

Law of specific energies 598716 389766 – statement as the common principle of sensory psychophysics, where each organ of senses has specific for its sensory modality independent from the character of acting irritant.

Substitute 514718 914 312 - directed from unconscious into conscious spiritual impulse, which is a new form of old repressed idea associated with incompatible desire.

Substitution 219618 918071 – process and the result of substitution of repressed drive or imagination with some other tendency or a signal; defensive mechanism, having different forms of manifestation. Results and marks of substitute are fault actions, some components of dreams, neurotic symptoms and etc.

Odor (smell) 289716 018 034 – sense determined by influence of smelling substances on receptors of mucous membrane of nose cavity.

Imprinting 298487 998194 – specific form of learning in superior vertebrates, when distinguishing features of objects of some inborn behavioral acts are fixed.

Memorizing 298761 519 314 – general name of active process, providing preservation of material in memory; enter of information in memory.

Spontaneous memory acquiring 519 612 81488917 – memorizing without intention to remember material and without usage of special means for better preservation of material in memory.

Voluntary memory 916899 001 –specified task with the aim of further reproduction or simple recognition, special act, which defines the choice of ways and means of memorizing and so influences its results.

Taboo (prohibition) 498716 398718 – attitude prescribing refusal of a drive reduction.

Contagion (emphatic contagion) 598 716 019 212198 – emotional contagion the process of transfer of emotional state from one person to other at the psychophysiologic level of contact except conceptual influence or additional to it in social psychology.

Shadowing 591814 – methodic procedure for research of auditory attention. It proceeds when a testee has to repeat orally a report, transmitting through one of some canals, and the canal is pointed by an experimentalist especially.

Learning 398 741 988 7191 – organized repetition of information with the aim to memorize it.

Defense 519481 979881 – complex of unconscious psychical processes providing security of mental health and a personality from negative dangerous and destructive inner psychic actions and external impulses.

Psychological defense 591069 51 – special regulatory system of personal stabilization, the system of mechanisms, aimed at minimization of negative experiences like elimination or minimizing of the anxious feeling associated with awareness of a conflict which puts at threat the personal wholeness. The function of psychological defense is the protection of the sphere of consciousness from negative and traumatic emotional stresses.

Psychological security 598061 319781 – relatively constant positive emotional feeling and awareness of an individual of ability to satisfy basic needs and assurance of own rights in any, even unprofitable situation, and when occurring of circumstances that may block or make it difficult to instrument them.

Sound: pitch 519381 998617- subjective quality of sounds, caused by their frequency. Sounds may be defined as low or high.

Mental health 519481913711 81 – state of spiritual (mental) well-being (sane mind), characterized by absence of painful psychic presentations and providing behavioral regulation and activity adequate relatively to conditions of reality. It is always reflected content of the notion consisted of regulating a spiritual man's life, social and group norms and values, medical or psychological criteria are considered as well.

Sign 519688 719317 019 – object or phenomenon used for the representative of other object, phenomenon or a process.

Knowledge 598764 019 82 – together with skills it provides correct reflection of natural and social laws, interrelations of people, person's place in a society and his behavior in notion and thinking of the world.

Knowledge: application 398781 499 511 – use of conceptual schemes for development of own activity. It requires the presence of already formed intellectual skills, containing special rules, according to which one must expand activity under new conditions. Processing of such skills is reached, as a rule, when educating by the way of problem situations' solving. The recognition of early acquired material in new situations, application of abstract knowledge is achieved by use of these skills.

Meaning(sense) 518761384871 – generalized form of reflection of social-historical experience, acquired in the process of common activity and communication; it exists as objective in the schemes of activity notions, social roles, norms and values. Through the system of meanings an image of the world and of other people represents for the subject's consciousness.

Zone (area) 598 511 689071 – space, characterized by certain common features.

Zone of development 517391 891489 – (zone of potential development) – 1. Abilities of psychic development opened with a minimum help the subject from outside. 2. Divergence at the level of difficulty of tasks, solving by a child aidless (level of actual development) and under control of an adult. The statement of zone of proximal development underlies processing by domestic age and pedagogic psychology of conception on correlation of teaching and mental development of a child.

Erogenous zone 59867106801 128 – certain parts and body areas such as genitals, oral cavity, anus etc. participating in development and functioning of sexual instinct; body places, playing role in achievement of sexual satisfaction. It possesses a special sensitiveness and is connected to some physiologic bowel and bladder habits;

their stimulation arises a pleasant excitement sexually colored.

Zoopragmatics 489061 968788 – a discipline, describing communication of animals as specific language from viewpoint correspondent to positions of pragmatics or more precise from the position of origin and mechanism of actions, fulfilling the communication of canals of the transfer of information (acoustic, tactile, optic, chemical) and the degree of ritualization of these actions.

Zoo psychology 398764 519812 – science of animal mentality, of manifestation and regularities of psychic evolution of animal mentality, of display and regularities of psychic reflectivity at the level. It considers problems of psi-development in phylogenesis and researches mainly under laboratory conditions the formation of psychic processes of animals in ontogenesis, origin of psyche and its development when evolving, biological premises and prehistory of emergence of man's consciousness.

Zoosemantics 489671 999 481 – the discipline, describing communication of animals as specific language from viewpoint of semantic, exactly from viewpoint of informative content of communicative actions, that may relate to the sphere of recognition, motivation of behavior and environmental relations.

Zoophilia 391517318 941 – love for animals, mostly erotic, when libido is turned to animals.

Maturity 398061 219 – the state when an organism is coming at an end of the period of development. It is to be the longest period of ontogenesis, characterized by tendency to achieve the highest development of spiritual, intellectual and physical abilities of a personality.

Prematurity 519488 079398 – spontaneous, untimed sexual maturity, that expresses violation, shortening or stop of infantile latent period and becomes the cause of diseases, provoking sexual manifestations, that may have perverse character and because of either unprepared state of genitals delays or undeveloped genital system.

Vision (eye sight) 588 061 989 711 – ability to

transform visual senses of energy of electro-magnetic radiance of light range (from 300 to 1000nm). When visual pigments of retina absorbs light quantum the visual excitement appears. Photochemical changes in retina pigments lead to changes of electric potentials which then are spread towards all levels of visual system.

Achromatic vision 518914 319 889 – loss of ability to differentiate chromatic colors. At that external world is perceived in grey color, which differs only by brightness depending on specter of perceivable light. Green color is perceived most brightly what is typical for twilight vision of people of normal color vision.

Binocular vision 518 617 998 227 – simultaneous formation of two images of one and the same object on the retina of two eyes to be one of the main mechanisms of perception of the space depth.

Spatial vision 598 061 788 610 – visual perception of three dimensional space. At that two main classes of perceptive operations are separated out, which provides constant perception: the first allows estimating of detachment of objects on the base of binocular and monocular parallax of movement, the second does to estimate the direction.

Mesopic vision 890 061 668 917 – (twilight vision) is to be the intermediate between the day and night vision.

Night (scotopic) vision 598 614 898 171 – it is provided through rod calls; at that only achromatic colors are perceived, but the light sensitivity is very high.

Day sight (photopic vision) 598 661 310 981 – is provided through cone cells, due to which the ability of color differentiation appears.

Chromatic vision 558 612 091 318 – ability to differentiate separately sub-range of electro-magnetic radiance in scope of visible specter (369-760 nm). Signals coming from peripheral sections of visual system in its highest divisions are perceived by spectrally-sensitive nervous cells, which are stimulated under the action of one of the colors of the specter and inhibited under the action of the other.

И

Iatrogenia 518 419 31798791 - It takes place as the result of incorrect actions of a physician, influenced on a client unintentional suggestive impact (incorrect comments of a disease), unprofitable changes of psychic state and psychogenic reactions, caused the appearance of neurosis. The synonym is a suggested disease.

Play (game) 518 006 78967 – individual activity, aimed at conditional modeling of some activity. It is the form of activity for a man under conditional situation, aimed at reproduction and acquiring of social experience, fixed in socially accepted ways of realization of objective actions, in objects of science and culture.

Game: development (pre-school age) 519 541 889 317 – process where child's play possesses the form of social learning.

Business game 598714 888 91 – the form of reconstruction of an object and social content of professional activity, modeling of the system of relations, typical for given kind of practice. Fulfillment of a role play is the proceeding of special (play) activity of participants on the imitative sample, reconstructing the conditions and dynamics of production.

Subjective game 598 71631 214 – children's game with subjects of material and spiritual culture or their substitutes, attached for control to cultural-historical peculiarities of these subjects and their immediate purpose.

Projective game 519387 918 499 – one of the projective methods which belongs to the group of methods of catharsis.

Role playing game 598741 389 618 – one of the elements of psychodrama when its participants play various roles which are significant for them in real life.

Children role playing game 518 781984 317 – dominate form of a game of pre-school age children where the modeling of actions and interrelation of adults occur. The role of adult, which a child takes, supposes the following certain often implicit rules due to which game actions with objects and interrelation with other children included in the game are regulated.

Symbolic game 598 748 918 3 – sort of a game where reality is reproduced as symbols or signs; the game actions are performed in form abstract symbolic.

Story game 598064 318 78 – children game where the story of real life, event, tales etc. are produced.

Story role-playing game 598421 319 816 – form of a game combined elements and features of story game and role playing game.

Idealization 819 816 917234 – Craving created private statement manifested in phenomenon of sexual overvalue of an object because the selected object was not been to some degree criticized and all his/her qualities were estimated higher than qualities of unpleasant people or than qualities of the same object while he has not been beloved.

Ideal 319448719 01 – special way of an object being, the presentation (active reflection) of in psychic world and life activity of a subject.

Identification 51948 01 216 – this notion is considered as the most important mechanism of socialization, revealing as individual's acceptance of the social role, when entering a group and being aware of group attachment, of formation of social attitudes and etc.

Group identification 819917 818 941 – identification of an individual oneself as the general image of a member of a social group or social community because of which it occurs taking of corresponding aims and values, often uncritical.

Collective identification 514217 219890 – It originates during activity as the common form of human relation, when feelings of one of the group are given to others as the motives of behavior, organizing their own activity, aimed at performance of the group aim and at elimination of frustrate impacts. It means unity of motivation and formation of relationship on the ground of moral principles. It fully expresses sympathy and cooperation when

© Grabovoi G.P., 2003

each group member emotionally and actively responds to successes and faults of every one.

Personal identification 598 067 918804 – the mechanism action of which is based on strong emotional tie of a person with other people, parents, leading to identification often unconscious with the 'other significant'. Guidance by other man as a model dramatically increases marks of social learning.

Narcissistic identification 5914 891087 019 – the process of self-projection towards an ego of lost sexual object when withdrawn libido is focused on ego, while a man relates to his own ego as to an abandoned object and direct towards ego ambivalent impulses included among others aggressive elements.

Gender role-playing identification 519719 89049 61 – the process and result of acquiring by a child of psychological and behavioral features of a person of a certain gender. It identifies psychological features and particulars of person's behavior of the same or opposite gender, including typical role behavior.

Identity 914 718518198641891 – the sense of self-identification of own truthfulness, usefulness, cooperation with world and other people. Sense of acquisition, adequacy and stable possession by a personality of own ego, independent from the changes of the latter and situation; ability to make full-fledged solving of tasks, which arise at each level of development.

Gender identity 519 488 714 317 – a person's consciousness of his gender belonging and experience of his/her masculinity or femininity; readiness to play certain gender role. Unity of self-consciousness and individual behavior, considering him/herself as a certain gender and focusing on the demands of corresponding gender role. It is one of aspects of personal identity based on imitation of parents.

Idea 54131 89 0168 – 1.Thought, general notion, presentation of an object or phenomenon, reflecting reality expressed as the attitude to it. 2. Defining notion, lying on the ground of theoretical system, logical construction, worldview. 3. Thought, intention, plan. 4. Mental image of something, notion of something.

Overvalued idea 591 811 01971 – statements, ideas, presentations, being marked in subject's consciousness as dominant position which does not correspond to their meaning. It is accompanied by expressive emotional feelings.

Idol 598061 789 12 - god, some object of worship, reverence with low manner.

Idolatry 5914 018 – 1.Worship of idols as religious cult. 2. Worship of some objects acting as idols, usually not subjected to reflection, slightly reportable.

Modern idolatry 598741 219 – Actually active widespread strong collective worship of power, success, market domination, including many hidden elements of various primitive religions.

Measurement 598 784 319 68 - In terms of psychology it is finding out of quantitative characteristics of researched psychic phenomena. In wide sense it is special procedure, when numbers (or simply ordinal values) are attaching to objects by certain rules. The rules consist in establishment of correlation between some features of numbers and some features of things.

Double image (ambiguous figure) 39148– an image permitting constituent elements' disconnection as subjectively perceived figure and background in a mutually opposite way; that is one part of the image is perceived as a figure, other one does as a background or vice-versa.

Isolation 498716 319 01 – Excluding of an individual from usual relations which may be observed under special conditions of work (space flight) or at clinic of nervous and mental diseases (insanity). Under such conditions side effects of isolation appear; loss of time orientation occurs; ability of thinking and memorizing are violated. Illusions and hallucination may be developed.

Group isolation 594 781 914 1 – Sort of

© Grabovoi G.P., 2003

psychological aspect it is a forced long existence of a group of people under conditions of limited space; lack of sensory irritants, constant communication with the same people. Under such conditions people stay at cosmic flights, when underwater swimming, at hydrometeostations and etc.

Perceptual (sensory) isolation 391819 016918 – sharp limitation of variability of usual sensorial experience such as visual, acoustic and etc.; partial or complete excluding of an individual from the flow of usual sensory experiences.

Complete isolation 519 816 418 – experimental method, through which the influence of isolation of a man is studied.

Illusion (sensory illusion) 589461 718 01 – inadequate reflection of an object and its attributes; perceptual aberration of private features of separate objects or images.

Aristotle's illusion 419 318 9164219 – consists in a small ball, placed between crossed index and middle fingers that is perceived as two different balls. It refers to tactile illusions.

Contrast illusion 584 171916 48 – distortion of partial features of objects appearing as damage of habitual stereotypes. It expressed as revaluation of attributes which are opposite to habitual, often as taste and temperature experiences. So, after cold a warm seems hot, after sour or salt the degree of sweet is revalued.

Moon illusion 5980614 318 – visual illusion, characterized by the fact that perceivable dimension of a cosmic body (Moon, Sun) seems larger when its position is low under horizon than when its position is high in the sky.

Oculogravic illusion 519 48171 – visually perceived movement, caused by influence of vestibular apparatus when increasing of an observer movement in the direction of vertical axis of a body. It is observed by pilots during and after a climb or descent: at the end of the climbing it seems that the object continues to move down, and after a dive recovering it does move up. Illusion may be expressed as distortion of objects' sizes, form and other spatial characteristics.

Optogeometric illusion 589 061 21 – various visual illusions, expressed as perversion of correlation of spatial attributes of visible objects. It is considered that they are determined by the action of mechanisms, providing constancy of visible dimensions and forms of objects. Most of illusions have tactile illusions in parallel.

Heaviness illusion 591 489 019 – corruption of perception of objects' weight attributes caused by former experience, if one lift two similar by weight but various sized objects, then the less one is perceived as heavier.

Image 571 48 12 – established for mass consciousness and characterized as a stereotype, emotionally colored image of something. A politician, profession, product etc. has a certain image.

Impotence 8851464 – sexual powerlessness. In terms of psychology it is interpreted widely applying to psychical phenomenon.

Psychic impotence 8985 419 81 – various disorders of sexual function, most of which has a simple inhibition nature.

Imprinting 918481 – a notion means rapid learning process during a brief perceptive period in early animals' life that established a long lasting behavioral features.

Impulse 519 514 819 – 1.Push towards something, stimulation to perform something, a cause invoked some action. 2. Electric impulse is fast short time jump of electric current or voltage.

Nervous impulse 489061 09817 - the excitement wave fast spread through nervous tissue appears as stimulation of sensory fiber of nerve endings, the fiber itself or nerve cell body. It is accompanied by fast change of excitement, conductivity or other features of a fiber.

Shameful surge 981317061 – the name of a psychosexual phenomenon, which further were named impulses.

Impulsiveness 488 01678918 – the feature of a nature, expressed as inclination to act without conscious control, under influence of outer circumstances or emotional experiences.

Non-punitiveness 489 068 719 – an inclination to rest responsibility for faults upon outer circumstances and conditions.

Inversion 489064 3197 -1. Process and result of replacement or substitution of motives, attitudes, desires, reactions, behavioral acts and etc. right up to opposite. 2. Type of gender orientation of men and women, when persons of the same gender are selected as the sexual objects.

Inversion: psychic mechanism 498711 619 8 – range of phenomena and psychic processes, causing appearance, development and action of inversion.

Invertere 489714 811 – the phenomenon which reveals some psychological qualities, characteristics in inverse or inverted form that is in the form in some sense and relation opposite to their normal shape.

Invertere absolutus 489641918 74 – the phenomenon of gender orientation towards an object of his/her own other than opposite gender.

Amphigenous inversion 489 7163194 (hermaphrodism psychosexual) the phenomenon of psychosexual orientation towards objects of own or opposite gender simultaneously.

Inhibition 488610 914 – the process and result of suppression, inhibition or even stoppage of some reactions, processes or activity.

Social inhibition 4897169184 –reducing (suppression), deterioration of productiveness of performed by an individual activity, its rate and quality when presenting of other people or observers, real or illusive (without intrusion in him/her actions), acting as a rival or observer for the actions. The phenomenon is opposite to social facilitation.

Index 488 617 01914 – a pointer, range of names and

etc. In terms of psychology it is numerical index for quantitative estimation characterizing of phenomena.

Sociometric index 4890 617 319 – the system of conditional definitions, numerical and letter, for quantitative characterizing of researched phenomena.

Individual (person) 48916 71913 – when a man is considered as a representative of hominis sapientis.

Individuality 489712 6148 – A man, characterized on the side of own social significant diversities relative to other people, peculiarity of psyche and personality of an individual and his uniqueness. It expresses features of temperament, nature, specific interests, qualities of perceptive processes and intellectuality, needs and abilities.

Individuation 499618 71809 – the process of a search of spiritual harmony, integration, wholeness, consciousness. The notion holds the central place in analytic psychology.

Indigo 498716 319 882 19 – ethno specific term means the syndrome presence of behavior regression with sudden change of consciousness and uncontrollable stimuli to eat human meat.

Indication 489 064 3191 – 1. The process and result of pointing to presence or absence of some state or process. 2. The process and result of reflection of a state or way of process or other object of observation, its qualitative or quantitative features.

Inductor 489614 719 – a subject, which addresses an information to a recipient. The synonym is communicator.

Induction 499711898418 – movement of knowledge from a separate assertion to general statements. It is tightly associated with deduction. Logic considers induction as a type of conclusion and differentiates of full complete induction and incomplete one. Psychology researches development and destruction of inductive reasoning. Movement from a separate to general knowledge is analysed under its conditioning of all psychic processes and structure of mental activity in whole.

Inertness 419517 31948 – the notion, used in psychophysiology to certain low mobility of nervous system, for which difficulties in transmission of conditional irritant from positive modus to inhibited and vice-versa are typical. Inertness for pathological damages (damages of frontal lobes) may occur as perversion.

Initiative 428714318 7 – a manifestation of the subject of activity not stimulated from outside and not ruled by independent circumstances.

Initiation 489614 7129 – complex of mainly ritual actions through which the change of social status of a person is performed and formally fixed; his/her inclusion in some close unity, acquiring of special knowledge, functions and rights occur.

Innervation 499617 81914 – producing of a nervous excitement in different organs.

Innovation 51931791814 – in social-psychological terms the creation and insertion of various innovations, originating of significant changes in social practice. There are different social-economic organizing, controlling and technical and technological innovations.

Instance 598614 319 7 (system) – the constituent of psychic apparatus.

Instinct 588914 31914 – complex of congenital components of behavior and mentality of animals and a man.

Self-preservation instinct 498175 61491 – inborn inclination and forms of behavior, aimed at adaptiveness for life conditions and for survival. Starvation and thirst belong to elementary instincts of self-preservation in psycho-analysis.

Sexual instinct 54 8 711 9 1 8 211

Integration 491619 881 89 —creation of inner unity, cohesion concerning intergroup process, which expressed collective identification, group cohesion as its whole-oriented unity, objectiveness in giving and acceptance of responsibility for successes and faults in joint activity.

Group integration 918517 918 48 – 1. State of a

group, characterized by: a) order of in-group structures b) correlation of main components of the system of group activity c) stability of subordinate interties among them d) stability and continuity of their functioning e) other features, witnesses of psychological unity and wholeness of social community. 2. Organized hierarchical range of in-group processes, providing achievement of the state. It is expressed as approximately unbreakable and autonomous existence of the group that supposes the presence of processes preventing damages of psychological preservation of a group. Absence of integrative features obligatory leads to disintegration of any community.

Intellect 419886 7198 – variously enough defined this notion though means in general individual features, corresponding to the cognitive sphere i.e. thinking, memory, perception, attention and etc. It is supposed a certain level of development of mental activity of a person, providing the ability to acquire new knowledge and use them effectively in life kind of ability to perform a process of cognition and effective problems' solving, in particular mastering of new circle of life tasks.

Intellect: structure 459618 71949 – its structure is described in factor-analytic theory, where 2 types of intellect are distinguished: 'fluid' which depends on inherent factors and displayed in tasks, where there is a need to adapt to new situations; 'crystallized' where the former experience is reflected.

Artificial intellect 498716 319 808 – 1. Conditional definition of cybernetic system and its logic-mathematic supplement, assigned for solving of some tasks, usually requiring the use of intellectual abilities of computers to solve tasks, earlier claimed obligatory human presence.

Practical intelligence 498016 719 78 – (senso-motor) – the notion to denote the stage of intellectual development in the period from birth to 2 years, preceding the period of intensive mastering of speech, during which the coordination of perception and movement is achieved. On

© Grabovoi G.P., 2003 111

this stage a child interacts with objects, their perceptive and motor signals but not with symbols, signs and schemes, representing the object.

Intellectualization 598716 3194 – defensive mechanism, which action is shown in specific way of analysis of problems set forward of a personality, that is typical by excessive overvalue of mental component when completely ignoring of emotional, affective and sensual components of analysis.

Intelligence 599617319 8 – range of personal attributes of an individual, responding to social expectations, which society demands towards a person of intellectual work and creation in wider aspect to people, considered as culture medium.

Intensity 598614319 819 – 1. Qualitative features, expressing the high measure, degree of a force, tension, density of some manifestation or process. 2. Qualitative or quantitative feature of power, tension, productiveness measure of a process or phenomena.

Intensity: relocation 498619 718 519 – one of psychic processes of a dream. In the course of the dream replacement of psychic intensity goes on, consisting in the processing when some important presentations and thoughts are deprived of the dominant meaning, others come to the foreground. It can be called a revaluation of mental values.

Intention 599 061 898719 – striving, directedness of consciousness to some object.

Paradoxical intention 489648 719 31 – psychotherapeutic method. It consists in a fact that client, obsessed by fear of expectation, receives from a logotherapist an instruction: in an emergency or before it happens to wish (phobia) for some minutes or to perform (compulsion neurosis) personally what he is afraid of.

Interactionism 59488 44 71931 – the branch of modern social psychology. Social interaction here is considered to be the immediate interpersonal communication (symbol exchange), important feature of which a human ability to 'take the role of other', to imagine how the partner or a group perceives him (generalized other), to correspondingly interpret the situation and to construct own actions is recognized.

Interaction 489 067 319 80078 – an interaction, influence of one on another.

Interview 488617 389016 – in terms of psychology the way to receive social and psychological information through the use of oral questioning.

Interview diagnostic 489061 71931 – the method to receive information of personal features, used at early stages of psychotherapy. It serves as the special mean to establish close personal contact with co-speaker. In many situations of clinic work it is an important way of penetration in the inner world of a client to understand his difficulties.

Interview clinical 519488 061714 089 – the method of therapy conversation in providing of psychological care.

Interiorisation 548 316 719 888 – the process of formation of inner structures of psyche, determined by acquiring of structures and symbols of outer social activity.

Interoreceptor 498617 319881 – sensitive nervous endings or receptors, perceiving mechanical, chemical and etc. shifts in inner environment of an organism. They are disposed in muscles, vessels, inner and organs.

Introception 519 814 319 889 – sensitivity of inner organs.

Interpsychological 591698 718 4 – interpersonal, occurring in psyche of several subjects, in interaction of psyches.

Interference 498617 889 511 – 1. Inter-suppression of simultaneously performed processes (related to cognitive sphere), determined by limited range of distributed attention. 2. Reduction of preservation of memorizing material as the result of influence of other material, with which a subject operates.

Skills interference 918488 712 81 – transfer of already produced private skills to new forming action on the base of their partial, clearly external similarity, what leads to difficulties in learning of new skills.

Proactive interference 549 316889 019 – the phenomenon of mnemic activity, consisting in reduction of preservation of learning material under influence of the material, learned earlier. It enlarges when extent of memorizing of interfering material and increasing of its volume, also during the growth of the extent of similarity of learning and interfering material.

Retroactive interference 898 764819 – reduction of preservation of acquired material, determined by learning or processing with the next material. Its relative value is decreased in the course of achievement of constant criteria of acquiring of primary material. It increases in the course of enlargement of similarity of the acquired and interfering material and achieves maximum in case of their coincidence.

Selective interference 488761 8 – the phenomenon of mnemic activity (memory), expresses delay of the answer to a question as the result of involuntary influence on it of word's meaning. Actually it acts at the solving of task to name the colors of letters of a word, especially if a word is the name of colors.

Intropunitiveness 916 071918 4- inclination to accuse oneself for all faults.

Introversion 498601 718 14 – frontage of a consciousness to itself, absorption at own problems and experiences, accompanied by reduction of attention to environment. One of the basic personal features. The opposite notion is extroversion.

Introversion 4986 01 718 14 (and extroversion) – the feature of an individual-psychological differences of a person, extreme poles of which correspond to the dominant direction of a personality or to the world of outer objects or to phenomena of own subjective world.

Introjection 4984 71 614 8908 – complete inversion by an individual in his inner world i.e. mentality of perceivable images, views, motives and attitudes of other people, when he do not differ own and other presentations. It is one of the grounds of identification, psychic mechanism, playing an important role in the formation of super-ego.

Introspection 891 698061 718 – the method of self-study, psychological analysis, research of psyche and its processes through subjective observation of the activity of own psyche. It consists in observation of own psychic processes without use of instruments or models.

Analytic introspection 898716 319 68 – an introspective method. It is characterized by striving to full portioning of a sense image into consisting components, not reduced to parameters of an irritant.

Systematic introspection 519481 918917 – an introspective method. It is characterized by orientation on tracking of the main stages of the process of thinking on the base of retrospective report.

Experimental introspection 914 891 618 378 – an experimental self-observation when a testee observes the dynamics of the experienced states at each stage of fulfillment of an instruction.

Intuition (insight) 489611 094 892 – often practically momentous finding of a task solving in lack of logical groundings; knowledge which appears without consciousness of the way and conditions of receipt of it as the result of immediate vision. It is to be interpreted as specific ability as whole grasp of conditions of problematic situations and as the mechanism of creative activity.

Infantilism 489618 719 31 – 1. Presentation in mentality and behavior of an adult of features, qualities, attitudes, inherent to childish age. 2. The form of delay, during the passing the stages of ontogenetic development, where physical and psychic functions are not developed. But the further possibility of full compensation of psychic development is preserved.

Personal infantilism 596 489 – preservation in mentality and behavior of adult features, inherent to childish age. An individual, who is tend to have intrinsic infantilism in process of normal or even fast physical and mental development is differed by immaturity of emotional-volition sphere what expresses dependence of solving and making actions, sense of non-defense, low criticism for himself, high demands for care, in various compensatory reactions (fancy, substituted real act, egocentrism etc.)

Informant 591648 718 – an involved in experiment subject which informs an experimenter (immediately or in written form) about specialties of his interaction with an object.

Informatics 8918 914 319 – 1. Science researching the process of transfer and processing of information. 2. Amount of branches of national economy which collects, transforms and uses the information. 3. Sphere of human activity. 4 Science researching processes of working with information by means of computers.

Information 419 317 819 209 – 1. Some news of environment and processes of it i.e. the object of preservation, processing and transfer received by a man or special devices. 2. News of the state of things, circumstances.

Information: parallel processing 498 714 318 218 9 – the model of processing of information in the brains, according to which the information has the set of transformations at certain 'functional blocks' of brains so that at the very moment of time its processing occurs simultaneously (parallel) in some 'blocks'. It is to be used in cognitive psychology.

Information: processing sequent 429 614 899 717 – the model of information processing in brains, when information in turn passes through the set of transformations in certain 'functional blocks' of brain so that at the very moment its processing occurs only in one 'block'. It is to be used in cognitive psychology.

Incest 348 617 - sexual relation (coitus) with blood relatives. Inborn erotic drive, aimed at parents (Oedipal complex) is one of the components of neurosis and wide spread form of sexual relations in primitive society.

Hypochondria 428 761 319 88 – painful state or a disease characterized by excessive attention to own health, phobia of incurable diseases, inclination to exaggerate pain, states and to ascribe nonexistent heavy illnesses to him/herself.

Irradiation 498 078 319 488 9 – capability of nervous process to spread from the place of origin to other nervous elements.

Apperceptive distortion 498 317918481 – any individual deviation from the standard interpretation of a stimulus.

Stagecraft 498 817 019 – one of approaches for cognition of a man. Reproduced actions of scenic hero under circumstances proposed by the author of a drama actor experiences 2 types of emotions: 1. Associated with success of his/her professional activity; 2. Similar to emotions of personality of part which he/she plays.

Fright 498317 918 - state of unexpected situation, sudden danger.

Testee 519317418 91 – a subject which undergoes psychological experiments; participant of psychological research.

Investigation (study) 529 311 488 07 – 1. Execution of scientific research. 2. Examination to clear out, to research something. 3. Scientific work.

Investigation: theme 318499614 – an aspect of a problem or separate question which is especially studied in given research.

Longitudinal study 419811 918 – long and systematic research of one and the same testees, allowing to define the range of age and individual change of stages of life cycle of a man; research of certain individual features of the same children during several years; where one can use methods of observation, experiment and test.

Pathographies' study 418917 2188 4 – a cycle of psychoanalytical studies.

Pilot research 481 912 – trial-search type of study

which is performed before the main one and which is its simple form. In social psychology pilot study is used to establish required scope of sampling, precision of a matter and number of test questions, time of questioning and etc. In testology pilot study (pre-test) serves the purpose of main test several standards revelation.

Field study 319 917 81944 – the type of study of social phenomena or behavior of animal communities through the study of them in normal natural conditions.

Psychodiagnostic research 488 718 918 41 – usually on its ground the hypothesis of dependence among various psychological features are checked up. It includes: 1. processing of demands for measure instruments 2. construction and approbation of methods 3. processing of rules of examination 4. processing and interpretation of results.

Psychological study 312 418 912 8 – search type supposes such stages: 1. formation of a problem; 2. suggestion of a hypothesis; 3. control of a hypothesis i.e. getting of empiric data and their processing; 4. interpretation of results.

Factor study 918 117 4889 018 (correlation study) - Studies of personality features. Their essence lays in possibility through the factor analysis of a large number of subjects to specify which personality features on the average were highly correlated with each other and which did on the contrary slightly. Positively correlated traits were the ones that most often tie together in one person.

Empirical study 489361 819 48 - a study based on the acquisition, analysis and synthesis of experimental (empirical) data.

Hysteria 5154891 – one of the types of neurosis, pathocharacterological disorder associated with excessive inclination to suggestion and self-suggestion and also weakness of conscious control of behavior. It is characterized by various disorders of mentality, motor sphere and sensitivity. It comes out in special hysterical character, convulsions and damages of consciousness and functions of internals.

Anxiety hysteria 891488 916 71 – the most frequent and first psychoneurotic childhood disease is 'childhood neurosis' which is predominantly developing in a phobia. Its psychic mechanism corresponds to mechanisms of phobias, excluding one point: when experiencing anxiety hysteria libido, liberated from pathogenic material through the ousting, is not converted. It does not transfer from mental sphere to corporal innervations but stay free as state of anxiety. It may be combined with conversion hysteria.

Historiography 498714 318 7 – 1. Science researching the development of historic knowledge, sometimes it uses as the synonym of history as a science. 2. The history of a problem research.

_Й_

Yoga 488 712 89901 – ancient Indian religious system of personal development associated with the system of psychological training, directed to the change of mentality through the high degree of concentration of attention.

_К_

Candaulism 489016681 9 – a type of sexual perversion, when a man receives satisfaction showing a naked woman or her photos.

Cancerophobia 209 488 6190 – neurosis, characterized by pathological fear of a cancer.

Caprice (whim) 523 488719 – a little whim, oddity without actual need, necessity.

Childish caprice 317988 9178 – a striving of children of pre-school and primary school age to do something opposite the adults prescriptions. It is often accompanied with cry or shout. Exhaustion, weakness of nervous system, high emotional excitement appear to be benevolent conditions for appearance of a caprice.

Cognitive map 488916 3194 – a subjective picture, having firstly spatial coordinates and images of situations of familiar spatial surrounding. It is to be created and changed during the active interaction of a subject with the world.

Inward picture of disease 318914 888 01 – arising in a patient's mind the whole image of a disease of him/her.

Ethnic world picture 521485 618 – unite cognitive orientation i.e. in fact non-verbal implicit expression of members' understanding of every society, ethnic community, of 'life rules', which social, natural and super-natural forces set. It is a scope of main admittance and suppositions, usually unconscious and indisputable, but directing and structuring of the behavior of the given community members, almost the same as grammar rules which seem to be unconscious for most of people, structure and direct their linguistic behavior.

Catalepsy 319 781 3194 - dreamlike state, characterized by low sensitivity to outer and inner stimuli, flexibility, involuntary preservation of any and all poses without visible efforts. It may show as hypnotic dream, also in cases of some psychic diseases.

Catharsis 488916 319 – primarily an emotional shock (strike), state of inner purification, evoked in the viewer of ancient drama as the result of experience for hero's fate, as a rule, ending in death. Strong emotional shock, evoked by not real life events, but their symbolic reflections in works of art.

Cathartic 4890 19218 – arising a discharge of psychogenic affects through the catharsis from reminding and recurrent experience of former events.

Categoriality 319681 0198 – the feature of perception, existing at the level of consciousness and characterizing the personal level of perception and the ability to separate out a certain areas in perceptive space, having more or less defined and constant limits. The precision of the limits is tightly connected to perceptive problems, which an individual has to solve.

Categorization 318916489 – a psychic process of classifying of a separate object and experience, either verbal or nonverbal meanings, symbols, sensory and perceptive models, social stereotypes, behavioral stereotypes. It is immediately included in the processes of perception, thinking, imagination, the object of which is perceived and understood not as a separate and immediate, but as a member of general class; it bears peculiarities of the given class of phenomena.

Cathexis 219488 0184 – 'energy charge', specific quantum of psychic and sexual energy.

Causometry 428911 3197 – the method of research of a subjective picture of life way and psychic time of an individual. It belongs to biographic method, aimed at the description of either former or supposed further stages of life way.

Speech kinesthesia 519488 914 31 – afferent impulses, going from peripheral organs of speech in cerebral cortex. It appear not only in outer speech activity, but in fulfillment of mental actions, when the tonus of speech muscles and appearance of motorial impulses because of hidden utterance of words may occur.

Claustrophobia 489317918 999 – a type of neurosis, characterized by pathological fear of closed spaces.

Bipolar cell 818 217 318 514 – a nerve cell, responsible for transfer of signals from cones and rods to ganglionic cells of retina.

Ganglionic cell 528 471 918 319 – nerve cells of retina, receiving signals from cones and rods through bipolar cells and transfer them to brain through visual nerves, formed by their axons.

Gliatic cell 498 378 019 481 – auxiliary cells of nerve fiber. Apparently they provides nutrition for nerve cells, some authors think they also take part in the formation of long-time memory.

Client 398617 891319 – a man seeking for psychological help. This term is more preferable than a patient which underlines the state of a disease.

Climate 3918998980171 – long statistic weather routine typical for a place due to its geographic position. In terms of psychology it is metaphorically widely used.

Social-psychological climate 390619 001798 (moral psychological group climate, atmosphere) – qualitative side of interpersonal relations, expresses the complex of psychological conditions, helping or disturbing for common activity productiveness and for whole development of a person in group.

Cliché 489617 318914 811 – superficial ways of behavior, stereotypic ways of interactions.

Cognitivism 489061 918715 - a direction in terms of psychology. It asserts that individuals are not only machines, mechanically response on inner factors or outer events, but it is available something more, than outer information for man consciousness. Cognitive approach mainly consists in a strive to understand the way a man decodes information of reality and organizes it to make decision or solve actual tasks.

'College invisible' 319 041899 017 — the unity of scientists, working in different offices and communicating through the use of personal contacts oral or written.

Collective 328677 918421 – a group joint by common aims and tasks of people, achieved during common activity the high level of development.

Collective: objective and axiological unity 598 716 388901 —- normative integration of individual activities in a group, when each activity, being functionally specific for the object or because of the way of its transformation and taking different hierarchical places in the system of the group activity, is mediated by the united axiological content of a subject of common activity. Such unity is the most important constituent of social group as general subject of activity.

Scientific collective: research program 378966 819716 918 – the ground and the way of organization of individual and collective activity, one of the key notion of social psychology of scientific collective. It originates from a problem situation, caused by logics of consciousness development, scientific and social context and unique life way of a scientist. It contains categorical, theoretical, operational, value-normative grounds of scientific activity, presentations of projected result and strategy of its achievement and etc.

Collectivism 589061 918 712 – expresses as a person's feature a man social development level revealed as personal responsibility for social progress and for collective, when participating in actions for social wellbeing. It is the principle of organization of interrelations and common activity of people, revealed whether private interests consciously subject to social ones; in cooperation, in readiness for interaction and help, understanding, tactfulness, interests towards problems and needs of each other.

Collective formation 588901 708961 8 – a stage of group construction meaning a transit of a group during common social-value activity from a low to the high level of development and finally to collective.

Coma 498716388917 – the damage of consciousness activity, characterized by absence of reaction to outer impacts, including pain irritants. At that pupils widen, the reaction to light is not fixed. Often pathological complexes appear.

Communication 491689 318712 – 1. The notion, close to the notion of communication, wider than it is though. It is the tie when the change of information between systems of live and not live nature occur.

Mass communication 518 555 948 71 – systematic spreading through copying mechanical means of specially prepared news, which have social significance, among numerous anonymous audiences to influence on attitudes, estimations, opinions and people behavior. Important social and political institute of the modern society acts as subsystem of the more complex system of communication, in wide scales fulfills functions of ideological and political organization, informing, education, entertainment. The institutional character of sources and delay of a backward tie between sources and audience is inherent to it.

Compensation 528916 388 917 – a reaction of an organism and mentality, opposing traumatic stimuli through the withdrawal of an active energy of all psychic system and creation of correspondent energetic density around the injured elements.

Compensation of functions 488716 318914 – the reconstruction of whole activity, damaged after falling out of some function from its structure. It occurs either on the ground of preserved function or reconstruction of the partially damaged functions.

Social-mental competence 589 411 399 01 – an ability of a person to interact effectively with other people in the system of interpersonal relations. It is formed during communications systems mastering by an individual and involving of him/her in common activity.

Complex 498764 388 91 – 1. The complex, combination of objects acts, features or phenomena on the whole. 2. Separate psychic processes' conjunction, which differs from the sum of its elements. 3. Specific interpretation is given in psychoanalysis, where it is considered as the group of psychic processes, united with the same affect, formed on the base of deep phylogenetic structures.

Castration complex 489068719317 – a specific childish response on the ascribed to father sexual threat or suppression of early-infantile sexual activity. Also it is the fear because of a penis (for a boys), the envy for a penis (for girls).

Masculinity complex 918617 399 814 - group of representation, collected mostly from jealousy, inferiority, and hope of a girl to find penis eventually and in the way to become equal to men. It brings great difficulties in the development of femininity. If the complex cannot be overcome 'the process of denial' begins in the spiritual life: the girl refuses to recognize the fact of 'castration' and believes she has a penis, and therefore has to act like a man.

Inferiority complex 498064 317 – leading to the neurotic deviation pathological syndrome, which consists in constant assurance of a man in own inferiority as a personality.

Complex of liveliness 489064 319 – the notion means various positive emotional-motor reactions of a baby in response to the appearance of adults, especially to mother's voice, her face, touch, or beautiful toys, pleasant sounds. It expresses as freezing-behavior, visual concentration on an object, smile, uttered sounds, motor liveliness.

Polycrates complex 491068 7143 – the notion, introduced in the frames of classic psychoanalysis for explanation of man's state, characterized by sense of worry, increasing when he achieves a higher life picks, and determined by unwillingness to be noticed by 'envy gods', and to lose all benefits.

Oedipus complex 488661 010 89 – the notion introduced in the frames of classic psychoanalysis that is immanent unconscious erotic childish drive to a parent of the opposite gender associated with aggressive feeling to a parent of the same gender. Appeared in the early childhood the complex of thoughts and senses, mainly unconscious, consisting in sexual drive of a boy to a parent of the opposite gender and the desire to physical elimination of a parent of the same gender.

Electra complex 914 668504 31 – the notion of psychoanalysis means unconscious erotic attraction of a girl to father and associated with the negative attitudes to mother.

Complex (combined, composite) 518477 39841 – expressing by itself the complex of something; enclosing the group of objects, processes or phenomena.

Compromise 5948981 819 47 – the defensive mechanism, provided only partial realization of painful impulses.

Convergence 319489481317 – collecting of a visual axis of both eyes on some object or a point of visual space.

Conversion 489716319 888 – the formation of a new word meaning: 1. or its transfer to a new paradigm of word-change 2. or its use in a context, different from traditional. It may be the reason of appearance of sense bearing barriers in communication.

Hysterical conversion 489715128 – somatic solving of a unconscious conflict; process, where for an affect, developed under pathogenic conditions, the normal discharge was closed and because of this the restrained affects have abnormal expression, or stay as sources of constant excitement, burdening of spiritual life.

Concretizing 48916171891 - filling of the general, schematic cognitive image of an object or of a situation with specific concrete features, so that it becomes possible to move forward the solving of concrete tasks.

Competition (rivalry) 558477 018 917 – one of the main form of organization of interpersonal interaction, characterized by achievement of individual or group aims and interests under the conditions of fight with other group or individuals, trying to reach the same aims. Usually it differs by strong personal involvement, activation of a subject of action, partial depersonalization of recept about a "rival".

Constancy 51438891817 (perceptual constancy) – regularity of perception, where it is seen the tie with specifics of irritants and psychological regularities. It is to be relative constancy, independence of perceivable features of objects in the change of conditions of perception. It allows keeping of constant features of objects, independent from a distance, angle and light with which they are perceived.

Physical build (constitution) 514 81291876 – joins some groups of features: morphological, bio-chemical, physiological – which in the aggregate, under significant influence of features of nervous system, constructs the base and the mechanism of a temperament.

Sexual constitution 518876 3184 – a type of sexual organization of an individual, at the time of forming of which the important part belongs to congenital components of sexuality. Various phenomena of normal and abnormal behavior are determined by the type of sexual constitution.

Personal construct 514889 316718891 – created by a subject the classifying-valuable model, through which the cognition of objects in their similarity and differences from others is realized.

Constructivism 5194886191 – cognitive development

is the result of sequent processes, consisting in consequent stages. Trying to understand reality a child constantly faces with new problems, destroying the already formed representations. This movement is defined by common influence of the mature of nervous system, experience of the play with objects and such factors as language and education. Inherited and so inherent to all is only the functioning of an intellect.

Consultation 584716319814 – 1.Advice, explanation of a specialist. 2. One of the types of learning studies i.e. a conversation of a teacher with students for widening and deepening of their knowledge. 3. Consultation of specialists on a question. 4. Institution which provides people with advices of specialists on practical questions or provides medical or health improvement care.

Professional advice 5847163 59481 – the strategy of psychological help for the individual in case of professional choice or planning of professional carrier.

Psychological counseling 7163489 488 101 – a form of practical psychological help as advices and recommendations on the ground of previous research of a problem of a client, also of research of clients themselves and their interrelations with people.

Contact-psychology 588 712989614 – the method of psychotherapy, based on the theory of psychic, where all inter human relations were originated from man-woman relation. For this method the therapeutic influence was directed mostly to realization of a client's ability for love often inhibited because of inadequacy and superficial contacts.

Contamination 489016 719 31 – 1. False reproduction of information, characterized by unifying of parts which belong to different objects in image or notion. 2. False reproduction of words, consisting in combination of syllables of different words in one word. Such substitutions may appear not only inside words, but in reproduction of lists of words, when words of one list are in other one. The sense and phonemic closeness of words helps contamination. In its ground there are phenomena of projective retroactive interference. As pathology it is observed for various memory disorders.

Context 489061 918 41 – having sense completeness, oral or written speech allows to create the meaning and sense for its separate fragments such as words, phrases, abstracts.

Content analysis 319488918 71 – in terms of psychology the method of revelation and estimation of specific features of texts and other carriers of information, where correspondingly to the aims of study the certain sense units of content and form of information are separated out: psychological features of heroes of news of human communication, types of people interrelation, genres etc. Then the systematic measurement of frequency and volume of notions of these units is performed, in different complex of texts. Content analysis allows to reveal separate features of a communicator, audience, news and their interconnection.

Counter-transference 489016 014 – unconscious transfer to a client's personality of emotional attitude of a psychotherapist towards significant other.

Contrast 489 618 – sharply expresses opposition.

Visual contrast 48741 31948 – visual estimation of approximate brightness or object's image lightness or its color in comparison with the background.

Brightness contrast 491 214 718 212 – brightness correlation of visual stimuli in one perception field. Minimum value of brightness contrast for simultaneously perceived objects is 1-2%, for successive it is not less than 4%. The range of contrast is 65-85% in practical tasks solving.

Control 514 318 718 48 – one of the perfect mechanisms of regulation of cognitive processes.

Social control 319 719 841 21145 – the system of ways of influence of society and social group on the person for regulation of his behavior and bringing to conformity with common standards in this society. It serves as the solving of a dual task that are achievement and support of stability of a social system and providing positive development of this system.

Cognitive contour 518914319 812 – subjective completion of a whole figure, constructed from separate fragments.

Fabrication 498716319718 – fault memories, observed in memory disorders.

Bitter candy 919 217819314 – conditional name of one of psychological and pedagogical experiments for children of pre-school and primary-school age.

Conflict 518716 319414 – collision of opposite targeted aims, interests, positions, opinions of opponents or subjects of interaction.

Conflict: typology 5889617889061 – In the capacity of main stimuli of activity two strivings are considered: 1. to achieve beneficial aim 'Appetenz –attraction' and to avoid unprofitable situation 'Aversion-disgust'.

Intrapersonal conflict 519 588961 499 1 – as a rule a source of ambivalent drives of a subject. In psychoanalysis the prior and constant form of the collision of opposite principles, drives etc., in which it is expressed the contradiction of human nature. It may be a form of interaction of contradictory impulses, of unconscious and conscious, of It and super ego.

Intergroup conflict 588961 531 8 – as subjects there are groups, following aims, incompatible with aims of the opposite group.

Interpersonal conflict 9 588961 481 – there are 2 forms: constructive and unconstructive. The unconstructive one appears, when one of the opponents resorts to moral condemnable methods of fight, try to repress a partner psychologically, to discredit him. Constructive one does when opponents do not come out of frames of business arguments and relations. There are different strategies of behavior there.

Neural conflict 898 01731844 – contradiction of a personality and significant for a person sides of reality, unproductive and irrationally resolved, what accompanied by appearance of painful heavy experience of failure, non-satisfaction of needs, losses etc. It is damage of important life relations of a man, activated in psyche traumatic situations.

Conflict organizational 588 418716 49 – collision of opposite targeted organizational positions of individuals or groups irrespective of aims of each other. It usually appears as the situation, when one needs to change sharply habitual type of activity (innovation), passes to new structure, conversion and etc.

Pathogenic conflict 86 8961 419716 – illness creative form of mental conflict, organized as the result of a fight between Ego drives and sexual drives, between ego and sexuality.

Constructive conflict 519 318 961 – the conflict, positively influencing on the structure, dynamics and result of social-psychological processes, serves as the source of self-improvement and self-development of a person.

Psychic conflict 519 688 8961318 – constant element of spiritual life characterized by unbreakable collision of drives, desires, mentality, systems and spheres of personality. When joining of superficially forced refusals from satisfaction of libido the conflict becomes pathogenic.

Ethnic conflict 588961919 61 – the form of intergroup conflict when groups with opposite interests are polarized on ethnic features. Their source is usually non-ethnic social and political and economic contradictions.

Conflict ego - Superego (ego/ego-ideal conflict) 491614 81 588961 – the form of reflection of contradictions of real and mental, outer and inner world.

Conformity 498617 91874 – submission of a man to real or illusive pressure of a group; expresses as change of his behavior and purposes correspondingly to primary not accepted by him position of the majority.

Conformity public 4 617 918897 481 – demonstrative submission to suggested by a group opinion at the aim to have an approval or to avoid reprimand or other sanctions from the group.

Conformity personal (inner) 179174 890101 – real

transformation of personal attitudes as the result of inner acceptance of the position of others estimated as more grounded or objective than own viewpoint.

Concentration 519688 01971 – an ability of the nervous processes to limit the sphere of own, spreading by primary source of origin; phenomenon opposite to irradiation.

Concept 901 67180161 – a content of a notion.

Concept figure 428917 0618901 – class of scientific presentation- schematic abstractions, as geometry figures, graphics of physical processes, structural forms of chemical substances etc., materialized in imagination. The name underlines their imaginative and notional nature.

Conception 90167 89 0619 – 1. System of views, knowledge of phenomena, processes etc. 2. United defining plot, lead thought of a work and etc.

Conception of detailed analysis 90167819481 – an idea developed in cognitive psychology on whether the recognition of a stimulus is provided through extraction of its inherent primitive features (lines, angles), on the ground of which the whole perception of a stimulus is built.

Conception of expressive motions 901 8954918048 – supposition that expressive human movements are the rudiments of instinctive actions of living creatures, joint by fight, attack, defense etc.

Conception dispositional 109817 61941899 – characterizes a personal behavior depending on states of its preparedness for a certain way of actions. Joint personal preparedness for the behavior in the given social situation with social conditions of previous activity, where constant disposition to realization of certain needs of a subject under corresponding conditions is formed.

Conception of mediated activity 498761 201891 – special social and psychological conception considering interpersonal relation in any sufficiently developed group as mediate by a content and value of activity.

Conception of the personal relations 901 678 5198 01

– a set of theoretical concepts, according to which the psychological core of personality is individual and integral system of its subjective, evaluative, conscious and selective attitude to reality which is to be an internalized experience of relations with other people in a social environment.

Conception of social representations 671 901 8984701 – one of the theories of 'middle range' aimed at revelation of tendencies of functioning of the structure of usual consciousness in modern society. The main idea of the mental structures of society must strengthen psychological stability of social subject and orient its behavior in changeable situations. The object of research is social reality as the complex of social presentations through which social relations are revealed in the individual consciousness.

Program role conception 67180 109 218 41 (program role concept of research team) – as to scientific collective the theory of research collective activity is considered in 3 interrelated aspects: logical, scientific and social and personally psychological. The unity of analysis of scientific activity is the research program, reflecting demands of logics of science development and is to be realized through the spreading of scientific roles among the members of the research group.

Conception of inner speech 901 180161 8980128 – theoretical model of the inner speech genesis from the so called egocentric speech, what is child's speech to itself out loud during a game or other studies.

Conception of self-organization 01 671918 4 – scientific direction appeared on the base of statistic physics, general theory of systems and cybernetics and structures' appearance researching regularities in unbalanced systems of not arranged elements. General principles of the self-organization are found out in physical, chemical, biological, social systems, but they are embodied most completely in high developed systems. In terms of psychology this conception may be spread with wide range of objects.

Stratometric conception 7180161489 – 1. Activity

conception. 2. Stratometric conception of a collective i.e. social and psychological theory of collective structuring. It is based on the supposition that dynamics of interpersonal relation in a social group may be interpreted only when considering of group processes' multi-level structure and defining of an intergroup activity levels' features.

Conception of levels of movement construction 901 671161 8901219 – concept according to which the construction of movements is understood as afferent ensembles taking place aiming to coordination of given movement and also for fulfillment of required corrections and for providing of adequate decoding for effectoral impulses, also all complex of system interrelations among them.

Conception of gradual formation 901 0161 519061 – the study of complex diversified changes, associated with the formation of new actions, images, notions of man's thinking.

Hormic conception 180161 8901791 – the moving force of individual and social behavior is the specific instinctive hormic energy defining the character of perception of objects, creating emotional excitement and orientation of mental and body actions of an organism.

Conception of specific energy 180161 8989 019 – the notion towards the fact that the quality of a sense depends on what sensory organ is stimulated.

Cooperation 0161 8989 01709 18 – one of the main form of organization of interpersonal interaction, characterized by joint efforts of members for achievement of a common aim in simultaneous division of functions, roles and duties among them.

Coordination 89019 880179 4901 – congruence, combination, putting in order of notions, actions, parts and etc.

Coordination reciprocal 8801791 917 – such interaction of nervous centers, when excitement of one center leads to inhibition of other one. So when exciting of muscles flexors neurons the activity of muscles extensors motor neurons is inhibited; when exciting of the inspiration centre the expiratory centre is inhibited.

Sensorimotor coordination 89019 8 901489 01 – coordination of actions and interactions of sensory organs and motor organs.

Koro 498716319 017 – ethnotypical term means the syndrome of a man accompanied by a feeling that a penis draws into abdominal cavity thus it is associated with the opinion that it must result in a death afterward. A neurotic fear up to a panic is typical for that.

Corporation 598617988719 – an organized group. Closeness, maximum centralization and authority of management, opposing itself to other social communities on the base of own narrow individualistic interests are typical for it. Interpersonal relations in a corporation are mediated by a-social and often anti-social value orientations. Personalization of an individual occurs through the depersonalization of other individuals.

Correction 498 067 2914 correction of some lacks which does not claim root changes of correcting processes or a phenomenon.

Psychological intervention 988061 2914 31 – it is considered to be an activity for correction of those specific features of psychic development, which do not correspond to the 'optimal' model on accepted system of criteria.

Preliminary correction 891617 498 067 – correction acts, included at moments about the origin of a movement and providing its fulfillment without faults. In mastering of a new movement the preliminary corrections change with themselves the secondary corrections, through which amendments were brought in the movement for incorrect movement performance. Increasing of objective action units and of conscious control release for other aims occur due to automation of preliminary corrections.

Cortical 918 8917 7015 – stemming from brain-cortex.

Indicator 499 718 801 – 1.In terms of mathematics it is usually a constant or known value serves as multiplier for other, usually variable or unknown value. 2. In terms of psychology it is often some numerical value, reflecting the degree of expression, development of a certain psychological quality or feature.

Intellectual quotient of 499 488 8017194 – intellectual quotient of or quantitative mark of mental development (IQ) is a relation of so called mental age VU to real (chronological) age VI of the given person according to the formula: VU/VI x 100% = IQ. Mental age is defined by results of tests with the help of one of age scale of an intellect.

Creativity 491817 3194 8 – creative abilities of individual i.e. abilities to originate unusual ideas deviated from traditional schemes of thinking, to solve problem situations quickly. Typical is a readiness to produce new ideas. It is constituent of the giftedness structure being an independent factor.

Crisis 8914 871 418618 –It is a state of mental disorder in terms of psychology, caused by long non-satisfaction of their own and interrelation with outer world.

Age crisis 14 871418918 – special rather short (up to a year) periods of ontogenesis. Sharp psychological changes are typical for it. It differs from crisis of neurotic and traumatic character and belongs to normative processes, necessary for normal, successive way of personal development. It may show transfer of a man from one age level to other, associated with system of qualitative transformations in the area of man's social relations, activity and consciousness.

Criterion 111888 9174819 – a measure; attribute, on the base of which estimation, definition and classification of something is performed.

Statistical criterion 891 4819 712 – indexes combining methods of calculation, theoretical distribution model, rules of making decision of zero truthfulness or one of alternative hypothesis.

Opponent circle 8901 31849141 – a circle of other significant, polemics with which regulates a creative activity of a subject. Revealing of the opponent circle is an important condition of social and psychological analysis of dynamics of creation, its dependence on interpersonal relations.

Cult 919 618719811 – worship of somebody or something; honoring of somebody or something.

Phallic cult 91618 7143191 – worship of male genital organ phallus as the symbol of fertility, life power in religions and traditions of some people.

Culture 91894219418 – 1. Complex of material and spiritual values, created in a society and characterizing the certain level of its development. 2. Level, degree of development, achieved in an area of knowledge or activity. 3. Degree of social and mental development, inherent in a person.

Culture: psychological area 4219418 – means of compulsion and ways called to reconcile people with culture and reward them for brought sacrifices.

Culture: stage 91894219418 81 4 – 3 stages of culture, characterized by development of sexual instinct and sexual morality are distinguished: 1. Level, where satisfaction of sexual sense does not pursue the aims of reproduction. 2. Stage, where all that does not serve the aim of reproduction is repressed. 3. Stage, where only legal reproduction is admitted as sexual aim.

_Λ_

Lability 498714 216 – maximal number of impulses which the nervous cell or functional structure can transfer in unit time without distortions. In terms of differential psychophysiology it is one of the main features of nervous system, cessation and onset speed of nervous processes characterized.

Lata 5910691 988101 – ethnotypical term means the syndrome, characteristic by damage of behavior in extreme situations: it unfolds according to the scheme of the repetition of actions, phrases, gestures of other people (echolalia, echopraxia), automatic performance of orders, stereotypic repetition of separate phrases. It occurs in the midst of sharp increase of excitement, hallucinations' onset.

Latent 491814 31916 – hidden, externally invisible.

Left-handedness (sinistrality) – 521614 9187128 – domination of the left hand which becomes the leading one because of inborn domination of the right hemisphere of brain.

Left-handedness hidden 614 91851481901 – formed skills of use of the right hand as the leading for left-hander by means of learning.

Laziness (idleness) 318 41791844 – the universal mean of defense from useless work. Often it is the effect of uncertainty of an aim, lack of stimuli, tiredness.

Treatment psychoanalytical typical 519317819478 – the complex and consequence of classic therapeutic procedures.

Falsity (mendacity) 9184117184 – an individual psychological feature, expressed as conscious distortion of the real state of things and also as striving to create wrong impression of facts and events. It contradicts the human demands emanating of the necessity to have the right image of society, actions and life circumstances.

Imaginary falsity 4117184 891618 – an inclination of a child to perceive events otherwise than how they are, but how he/she wants. A child fancies identifying himself/herself with other people e.g. with heroes of tales. Often it is revealed for 4-5 year old children and it is over when he/she outgrows.

Libido 5986179184 91 – a theoretical notion has been calling for explanation of the psychic life dynamics on the base of analogy with energy, as it was interpreted at physics; one of the key notion of psychoanalysis.

Libido: fixation 179184 98 218914 – fixation of libido on this or that element; predisposed inner factor of aetiology of neurosis.

© Grabovoi G.P., 2003

Leader 418914 318 718 – a member of a group, to whom all other members give the right to make responsible decisions, touching their interests and defining the direction and the character of group activity. The most authoritative personality which really plays the central part of activity organizing and group interrelations' regulation.

Leadership 318 788 914 6819 – the relation of domination, subordination, influence and complying in the system of interpersonal relations in group.

Leadership: style 91418718 519 –the typical for a leader system of ways of influence on his subordinates.

Line of sight 891489016718 – a line joining together a pupil with the point of sight fixation on an object. From ergonomic viewpoint optimal observation is achieved on the line of sight with 15 % of decline downward to the line that is parallel to the earth surface.

Hypocrisy 489016 917 81 – a behavior, covering insincerity, evil aims by false virtue, frankness, false good aims.

Hypocrisy cultural 9016 917 489 1 – a special state supported by a society due to inherent sense of uncertainty and the need to defend own actual liability by prohibition of criticism and discussion. It appears because of the fact that society claims fulfillment of high ideal of morality for each member of society regardless of how difficult is it.

Personality 498617 218191 317 – a phenomenon of social development, the concrete living person owned consciousness and self-consciousness. Structure of personality is a whole systematic structure, complex of socially significant psychic features, relations and individual actions, formed in the course of ontogenesis process and defining his behavior as the behavior of the conscious subject of activity and communication. Personality is the self-regulated dynamic functional system of constantly interacting features, relations and actions, forming in the course of human ontogenesis process. Personality is the self-drive self-developing system, which comes to the higher level of its consciousness during its development.

Personality: activity 8617191 317 912841 – the ability to produce socially important transformations in the world on the ground of acquiring of resources of material and spiritual culture. It is expressed as creativity, acts of volition and communication. Its integral feature is active life position.

Personality: psychic apparatus 617 2191 317217 91 – consists of 3 areas (regions) or 3 kingdoms: Super ego, Me, It, and also of the system of their interactions.

Personality: research: method 17 21817 788 – the complex of ways and methods of personality manifestations' psychic research.

Personality: research: standard method 191 31897 91481 – created on the base of multiphasic Minnesota personality inventory MMPI considering the norm of mentality grasp research.

Personality: orientation 617191 317 8914 81 – its integral and general feature. The complex of constant motives, orienting of personal activity to relatively independent from the current situation. It is characterized by interests, inclinations, ideals of a person, reflecting his world view and expressed as the harmony and non-contradiction of knowledge, relations and dominating motives of behavior and personal actions. It expresses world view, spiritual needs and practical actions.

Personality: sensory organization 8817 218919481 – the level of psychological functioning of analyzers' system and individual features of their combining as complexes. It is bound to basic psychophysiologic features of an organism i.e. to the type of the highest nervous activity and temperament; level of thresholds of perception is separated out as one of criterion of relation towards this or that temperament; levels of development of sensitivity are the properties for the development of abilities.

Personality: development 218191 317 489 – the process of personal formation of an individual social quality as the result of his socialization and education. Having natural anatomic and psychological predispositions for personal growth during socialization a child comes into interaction with the world when acquiring achievements of mankind. Forming in the course of the process, abilities and functions reproduce the historically created human qualities of a personality. Mastering of the reality by child is realized during its activity with help of adults, that is why the process of education is the leading in personal development.

Personality: epigenetic development 172819117 519 – constant development process of 8 stages from the babyhood to oldness, where each stage is a special alternative phase of solving of the age and situational tasks of development.

Personality: self-definition 191 317 989801719 – a conscious act of reveal and assertion of own position in a problem situation. Its special forms are collective and professional self-definition.

Personality: type 8191 317 891 – as the basic criteria, when one can classify people into certain types.

Personality: formation 172181 9117 891 – objective and regular process, when a man acts not only as an object of influence but as a subject of activity and communication.

Personality: character 191317 498 014 – Expressing in short the essence of differences between a personality and character, one can say, the features of character expresses how an individual acts, his personal features and that for the sake of what he acts. Actually the way of behavior and personal direction are relatively independent that is when using one and the same way one may achieve different aims and, vice-versa, a person may achieve an aim by means of different ways.

Authoritarian personality 498617218 214 – the notion and conception, describing the special type of personality, that is the base of totalitarian regimes. It is characterized by: intolerance of freedom, craving of self-assertion and power, aggressiveness, orientation on authority of a leader, group, state; stereotype in thinking and conformism, hatred to intellectual and people of other ethnic group etc.

Personality criminal 218191 3178 – in terms of juridical psychology it is the complex of psychological features, typical for persons making crimes.

Referential personality 18191 381876 – a man especially important and valuable for other as a model to emulate. He/she is referential for those on whom he or she makes a strong influence. He/she acts as a source of basic values, norms, rules of behavior.

Self-actualizing person 191 317 481901 – a man achieved the level of self-actualization. Is to be special, not burdened by small sins as envy, cynicism, hatred etc; not inclined to depression, pessimism, tolerant to other, independent from conventionalities; simple and democratic who has a sense of humor of philosophic character and also inclined to experience of pick senses like inspiration etc.

Deprivation 519488918 417 – a state, inserted through the refusal and appeared due to a taboo.

Logos 319481919617819 – the term of ancient Greek philosophy, which means Cosmic Intellect, Sense, Word, Law, Speech, ground of the world, its order and harmony. According to S.Freud it is the symbol of human intellect.

Logo therapy 3196178198 916 – one of the directions of psychotherapy the psychotherapeutic strategy, based on the supposition, that personal development is determined by the striving to search and realization of meaning of life.

Falsity (lie) 319 814 71978 – the phenomenon of communication, consisting in special distortion of real state of things; expresses a content of speech, immediate control of which is difficult or impossible. It expresses itself as conscious product of speech activity, having the aim to mislead recipients (audience).

Biolocation 421 78806418 – finding out through the use of special indicator of sub-earth water, cavities etc. It can be a rod, a pendulum, a frame and etc. for an indicator.

© Grabovoi G.P., 2003

Localizationism narrow 318 614 818 9 – neuropsychic direction, where psychological functions were considered as unite, indispensable of composition parts psychic abilities, realizing through the work of narrow localized parts of brain.

Local 489712698 01 – local, typical for a given place, keep within certain limits.

Locomotion 391 688 6054321 - for animals it is movement, active displacement in space: scrawling, walk, run, swimming, flight etc. It is characterized by example of firmly programmed and fixed in a gene of inborn motion coordination, consisting of the base of instinctive components of animal behavior.

Locus of control 318491219 067 – the notion, characterizes the localization of reasons, by which a subject explains his/her own behavior and behavior of other people.

Love 888 412 1289018 - the high degree of emotionally positive attitude separates out its object among other and place it in the center of life needs and interests of a subject: love for motherland, mother, children, music, etc. Intensive, strained and relatively constant feeling, psychologically determined by sexual needs; expresses socially formed drive to be maximally full represented by own personally significant features in life activity of other, so that in order to stimulate in him the need in backward feeling of the same intensity and stability.

Eternal love 888 912 818848 – the love differed with the singularity of subject's consciousness towards the factor of falling in endless love. It is characterized by decision to live and develop eternally and the possibility to realize it on the ground that eternal love is eternity objectively realized for a subject.

Love: types 888 12418 316019 – various displays of love dependent on an object: 1.Brother love (agape) the fundamental type, composing the base of all types of love 2.Maternal love, 3. Erotic love, 4.Love for ourselves, 5. Love for God.

Love: condition 2 128901468 – components of male type of choice of a sexual object of love life. It is characterized by 1.Position of the 3rdvictim 2. Love of prostitutes 3. Drive to women, close to the type of prostitutes as the most valuable objects of love 4. Tendency to rescue the lover, expresses that a man does not leave her, because he is sure that his lover needs him, and may lost the moral support and come down to low level without him.

Inhibited love 219888 412 1289018 – distinguishing character of inhibition relative to the aim of love.

_M_

Masochism 389 216 489011 – the notion, means sexual perversion, characterized by tie of sexual satisfaction with the obligatory experience of moral and physical sufferings. Sexual satisfaction of masochism is achieved from application of physical impacts on him, abuse and others from the partner's side.

Macropsia (megalopsy) 318419 614 717 – subjective extension of visible dimensions of distant objects. It appears when damaging of sincipital and occipital sections of visual analyzer, but observed also in the norm, when an individual makes efforts to decrease the accommodation of an eye.

Manipulation 489061 718 4 – manipulation and manipulative solving of the tasks give especially deep, various and essential for psychic development data of an object's components of environment and processes in it.

Masking 488 616 001 919 – the process and result of an action, devoted to making invisible for somebody of something or somebody.

Visual masking 816 001 919 814 – reduction of recognition of attributes of a stimulus (actually perceivable subject), when it is shown the other stimulus which can: 1.to act at the same time with the main one (simultaneous masking) 2.to precede it (forward masking) 3. to follow it (backward masking).

Masculinity 5147 18 28 –the complex of

© Grabovoi G.P., 2003

psychological and characterological features, traditionally ascribed to men. The power, strength, determination, hardness and etc. belong to them.

Masculinity 51471828 (masculinity and femininity) - normative view of a physical, mental and behavioral characteristics, typical for men and women, the element of sexual symbolism associated with the differentiation of gender roles. In differential psychology masculinity and femininity are specific scientific constructs associated with specific psychodiagnostic tests.

Mass 488 91801517 319 (psychology mass) – community of people, where there is a libidinal attachment either to the leader or among individuals. Sometimes it is called psychological mass. Masses are differed from simple meeting of people. It is subdivided into natural and artificial masses.

Mass: libidinal constitution 80151739 319 (libidinous mass constitution)– 'primary mass' which has the leader and has not the quality of individual; some amount of individuals, who made the one and the same object to be their Superego and so were identified among themselves in their Ego.

Homogeneous mass 517 319819495 01 – psychological masses, consisting of homogeneous individuals.

Artificial mass 1517 319 48 – highly organized, long existing communities such as church, army. Their formation and functioning is realized with some violence.

Masturbation 0021421 – a sexual self-satisfaction, achieved by stimulation of erotic zones or psychological excitement, when sexual fancies lead to the experience of orgasm without any and all manipulations.

Matrix 819 319 06018 – in mathematics orthogonal table of some mathematic objects: numbers, math expressions etc. In terms of psychology the notion of the term is similar, but instead of math objects there are some psychological objects for instance tests.

Raven's Progressive matrices 06018914 318417 – a set of tests for the diagnostics of an intellectual level. It is based on the work of obvious (objective) thinking on the analogy.

Emotional matrix 819 3199813191 – a form of existence and expression of thoughts, reflecting real senses and convictions and defining of man's actions.

Meditation 9188013210617 – intensive, deep-drawn penetrating thinking, immersion by an intellect into object, idea etc., achieved through the concentration on the object and elimination of all factors inner (light, sound) or external (physical, emotional and others), distracting of attention. The method of psychic training, taking various forms dependent on cultural-historical environment.

Medicine psycho-somatic 529 321 688 17 – a branch of medicine, based on the acceptance of exceptional dominant or special role of psychic factors in appearance, development and outcome of somatic diseases.

Melancholic 489614 318171 – a subject, having one or 4 main types of character. This man may be characterized as sensitive, inclined to perceive deeply even little faults, but visibly inertly reacting on environment. It *is* characterized by low level of psychic activity, slow motion, speech and quick exhaustion.

Melancholy 614 318171 8914218 – pain state, expressed as suppressed mood, slow movements and difficult thought flow.

Work place: learning field 481816 719317 – subjective space of a human operator, where key sources of signals about operations in the process of activity are placed.

Metapsychology 8914819 3198714 – psychology, describing psychic processes with regard to dynamics, topic factors and economy.

Metasimulation 48181941 89 – prolongation of the symptoms of a disease already presented earlier.

Method 919 411 819 311 (research method) – 1. Technique, way, image of action. 2. Way of cognition, the research of phenomena of natural social life; way of practical realization of something. Way of organization of an activity, grounded normative way of realization of scientific research. Way of research, flowing out from the general theoretical presentation of the essence of the studies' object.

Method: analysis of life way 489316 718 444 – one of the leading methods of psychological correction, based on joint analysis of client's life way and definition of realistic life aims – without deep processing of emotional problems.

Association method 398716 818 (method of free associations) – therapeutic way of Freud psychoanalysis, when it is proposed to a client to say freely everything that comes into his head. It is supposed that a client, unconsciously, may blab out; to utter words spontaneously, that point at involuntary appearing thoughts; analysis of these thoughts and associations point the reason and source of his disease or excitement.

Biographical method 488 712919316 – ways of research, diagnostics, correction and projection of the life way of a personality.

Co-twin control method 391 614 818917 – the strategy of research which is the most informative among psychogenetic methods. It is based on the premises, that environment influences on twins in just similar way. It allows judging of the influence of genetics and area factors on the studied psychological quality and on variety of researched features. It is characterized by comparison of psychological qualities of the monozygotic twins having identical set of genes and of dizygotic twins whose genotypes are different and have only 50% of similar genes.

Method of active imagination 428 614 9187168 – the main method of psychological correction in Carl Jung therapy. It supposes the ability of facing and interaction with the symbols of unconscious.

Method genealogic 918616 391711 – belongs to psychogenetic methods. Here the research of similarity among relations of different generations is performed.

Method genetic 498061 718919 – the method of study of psychic phenomena in development, clearing out the origin and laws of transformation in the process of development.

Method of adopted children 808 417 318 – psychogenetic method, allow to judge of genetic and area factors' influence on the variety of studied features through establishment of the similarity of an adopted child with his/her biological and adopted parents. The ground there is a comparison of similarity of some psychological feature between a child and biological parents, and a child and his adopters.

Method of group discussion 418917 318919 – 1. Used in practice of management of collectives, the way of organization of joint activity, aimed at intensive and productive solving of a group task. 2. Technique allowed to influence on the opinions, positions and attitudes of members of the discussion in the way of communication using the system of logically grounded reasons.

Method of semantic differential 8918 51981891 – associative procedure is the one of the methods of construction of semantic subjective spaces. It is used in studies associated with man's perception and behavior and with analysis of social attitudes and personal meanings; in terms of psychology and sociology and in the theory of mass communication and advertisement and also in esthetics.

Method zoo-psychological 489617 319818 918 – ways of study of animal behavior, including observation and experiment.

Method of minimum changes 898716319418 – the method of definition of the threshold of perception, when it is performed the monotonous step-by-step change of a value of acting irritant till the point of appearing and the point of disappearance of senses is defined.

Method of psychiatric interview 891617 318917 – the main method of psychological correction. The main attention is turned to the 'general emotion' appearing in a therapeutic situation between a doctor and a client.

Historical method 891 811 9187 16 - the method of

studying the phenomena of mental development, revealing their dependence on the historical conditions of life.

Method of cardiogram 889 317 48678 – the method of registration of biological activity of heart muscles, applied in terms of psychology for the analysis of vegetative shifts.

Cathartic method 499 818 906714 – the method of psychotherapy, devoted to the treatment of some psycho-nervous diseases. Its main provision is that symptoms for hysteric men depend on shocked them, but forgotten scenes out of a life.

Complex method 980491 716 318 – used as the organizing. Here it is used the other reason for the method classifying: so, comparative and longitude methods may be or may not be complex. That is, the research may be performed in the frames of one science or as the complex interdisciplinary researches.

Longitude method 48871631944 (longitudinal method)- relates to organizing methods. It supposes the work with one and the same group of people or with a separate man regularly and rather often observing them during long time to follow the development and to use 'the longitudinal section'.

Luria method 498 71431871 – the set of neuropsychological methods serving for diagnostics of local damages of brain towards corresponding psychic damages. They are the set of test probes of different cognitive processes, voluntary actions and personal features.

Method of myogram 489617814312 – the method of registration of heart muscle bioelectrical activity for estimation of intensity, localization and timing parameters of muscles movement, e.g. for hidden movement reactions' registration.

Method of participant observation 498061 7189174 – the method of study of social-psychological processes in small groups, where the experimenter takes part of his own, observing as if from inside or outside at once.

Method of objective observation 489614 31842 – the

strategy of research for fixation of the given characteristics of a process without interference in its flow. It may be guided by registration of behavioral acts and psychological processes. As a rule, it acts as preliminary stage before planning and fulfillment of experimental research.

Objective method 489614 918 8 – the strategy of analysis of psychic content, maximally oriented on other object (not as for introspectionism towards itself) and use of verifying hypothesis. It relates to organizational method.

Descriptive method 498614 718 – a researcher acts as an observer here: he never interferes with observed phenomenon being limited by utmost possible objective descriptions.

Q method 219618 71481901 - they are: 1. Talk; 2. Questionnaire; 3 Interview.

Organizational method 498614 718 7819 – they are: 1. Comparative method and method of sections as its special case; 2. Longitude method 3. Complex method 4. Objective and subjective methods.

Method of assessment program 491718 51431 (method of expert evaluation, method of external expert evaluation)– the method of psychodiagnostics, supporting by opinions of experts which know profoundly the estimating phenomena and can give it objective mark. It supposes a rcsearch and generalization of opinions of all experts. It is widely used in personal psychology.

Polyeffectoral method 9189181417418 4 – it uses simultaneous registration of some reactions of an organism in response to the action of an irritant. Such psychophysiologic marks are often registered for this mode as following: skin-galvanic reaction, brain secondary, vibration, myographic reaction, breathing, blood pressure.

Method populational 319617 919 81 – relates to psychogenetic methods. Allow to research the spread of separate genes as chromosomes anomaly in human populations. For analysis of genetic structure of population there it is studied a large group, that must be representative.-

/this method is also informative in the study of inherent pathology.

Evoked potential method 498617 319 489 —Method of registration of bioelectric activity of the brain, changes of which are caused by external influences and are reflected in the relative temporal proximity to this effect. In particular, you can explore the rhythmic fluctuations of biopotential in response to the externally imposed rhythm of the stimulus. On the basis of the data obtained with the help of this method, the hypothesis about the mechanisms of perception, attention, intellect, about hemisphere asymmetry of the brain and of the individual psycho physiological differentiation are framed.

Trial and error method 498617 319 - the kind of learning as a way to develop new forms of behavior in problem situations.

Projective method 319614819 8 – one of the methods of personality study. It is based on exposure of projections in the given experiments with their further interpretation.

Method of dichotic listening 448618 319 48 – the method, devoted to analysis of selective attention and asymmetry of brain hemispheres. It is characterized by simultaneous display of different stimuli for the right and left ears.

Method of polar profiles 4986179184 – the way of description and evaluation of studied objects such as notions, social attitudes, stereotypes with the help of the set of bipolar scales, given by the contradiction of adjectives, nouns or detailed speaking (hard-soft, cold-warm etc.).

Psycho-genetic method 498716 3194 – the method allowing to define influence of inherent factors and environment on formation of psychic features of a person. They are: twin method, genealogic method, population method, method of adopted children.

Psychodiagnostic method 498617 3194 8178 – the method of reveal of individual features on the base of procedures, proved their effectiveness.

Method of semantic radical 498612 7194 – one of the objective methods of experimental semantics for definition of semantic fields. It consists in the analysis of a meaning through detachment of their associative fields. On the base there is a process of formation and transfer of conditional reflects for the definition of semantic closeness of objects. As a criterion of semantic closeness there used the transfer of conditional-refectory reaction of one object to other, semantically associated with it.

Method of skin-galvanic reaction 498617 3194 – the method of registration of bioelectrical skin activity as a mark of involuntary vegetative activity. It is used for evaluation of a change of functional state, orientation and emotional reaction as well as personal differences.

Method of reference estimation 918716 319 48 – a methodic technique, a way of reference display of group members for every individual entering. It contains 2 procedures. When processing of preliminary one there are separated out positions (opinions, values, attitudes) of every group member of an important event, a man or an object with the help of questionnaire list. The second procedure reveals a person, whose position, reflected in the list, is the most interesting for other testees. It forces a testee to show high selectivity towards persons in the group, whose position is especially actual for him/her.

Method of psychological self-regulation 498612 719 481 – the system of learning, directed to formation by a subject of inner means of the control of own states. There are types of such methods: nervous-muscles relaxation, auto-training, ideomotor training, imaginative, meditative methods, and autohypnosis. Learning of the method is especially successful under conditions of specially organized cycles of study.

Blind method 489317 889 41 – supposes elimination of distorting of an experiment artifacts associated with the fact that a testee knows what is studied and what is expected from them. Though knowledge of researchers about the same may be noticeable either. So, the dual blind method was introduced in practice.

Sociometric method 498 051 618421 – a diagnostic method serves for analysis of interpersonal relation in small groups. When using it each member is questioned and after response it makes consequent choice and ranging of other group members. Usually there are questions about group members preferable in some or other situations.

Method comparative genetic 488 617 319 81 – research strategy, used for the study of regularities of psychic activity through comparison of qualitatively especial stages of its development.

Comparative method 498 617 3198819 – it is widely used in all spheres of psychology. It is realized for comparison of psychic features on different stages of evolution. In terms of ethnopsychology it is embodied in the reveal of psychological features of different people. In developmental psychology it acts in the capacity of the method of cross-sections and it is opposed to the longitude method. Both of them are directed to the definition of features of psychic development relatively to age in different ways though.

Cross-sectional survey 419 6173184 - relates to organizational methods. Research is organized as the work with people of different ages similar to performance of cross-sections at different age levels. When it is sufficient quantity of members of each group one may reveal common features at each level and follows the common tendencies of age development on this base.

Statistical method 31947 819 448 – in terms of psychology it is some techniques of compulsory mathematic statistics, used mainly for processing of experimental data. The main aim of the usage is increase of grounds of conclusions in the study due to use of probability logics and probability models.

Subjective method 498617 818 911 – it presumes

that the object, with which a psychologist interacts, is himself/herself as an observer and the patient which is observed, experimenter and a testee. This method is often associated with the notion of introspection or self-observation. It supposes the turn of the psychologist to his inner experience and a trial to catch changes in own psychic life under different conditions.

Scaling method 219317 41918 – the method provides application of qualitative indices for estimation of testee relation with certain objects, which can be physical or social processes. For performance of subjective scaling there are techniques characterized by certain rules through which numerical estimations are prescribed for certain objects features. Method of average error, method of minimum changes and method of constant irritants are used in the frames of classic psychology.

Experimental method 498614319 819 – it may appear to be similar to method of introspection, it has essential differences though: 1. You take for experiments inexperienced relatively to self-observation specialist kind of 'naïve' observer and the less he/she knows psychology the better 2. It is required from a testee a common report of perceived things in those terms, which he uses daily rather than analytical one.

Electrophysiological method 817319 41849808 – methods of organic systems' activity analysis on the basis of registration of biopotentials, change of which may occur spontaneously or in response to the external irritant. Brain action currents at that are analyzed by encephalogram and induced potentials; it must be made by myogram for muscles; the same process for skin is to be made by skin galvanic reaction and for heart it is making by cardiogram.

Method of encephalogram 519617 3194 80817 – method of registration of electro biological activity of brains at different parts of scalp surface. It serves for analysis of cerebral activity changes in various experimental situations. On the base of data of psychological processes hypothesis of the work of various psychic processes are built included perception, attention, thinking, memory, emotions, motions, speech and self-regulation. More than that, due to existence of constant individual features of encephalogram this method may be used in differential psychology and psychophysiology.

Technique (procedure, methodology) 319418614 3 – 1. Complex of procedures, methods of learning of something, methods of expedient performance of a work, process or practical fulfillment of something. Technical procedures of realization of the method at the aim to clear up and to verify knowledge of studied object. 2 Practical fulfillment of the method as elaborated technique of researched subject and object interaction organization on the base of certain material and concrete procedure. 3 Science of learning methods.

Methodology of pair associations 519 314 819 8 – method of memory study, where after the memorizing of list of pairs of stimuli (senseless syllables, words, pictures) by a testee he is given a task: after next presentations of every 1 element of a pair to reproduce the 2nd element.

Unconscious methodology 498617 919 016 – method aimed at reveal of unconscious reactions, e.g. projective technique.

Blank methodology 489614 314 81 – a procedure, where series of reasoning and questions are proposed to a testee to which he/she must answer, orally or in writing; at that special blank is filled, where these answers are fixed by a testee or by the person asked. The answers show judgments of testee psychological features. Wide use of such procedures and practical interest to them are explained by their working out and processing of results simplicity.

Methodology of partial reproduction 419712 81914 – a procedure for a study of iconic memory. It is characterized by the fact that a testee gets the instruction to reproduce only the part of information, shown for short time. Pointing out of what namely one must reproduce is performed by light or a sound signal, which is given with some delay after presentation of a material for memorizing. It was shown with the help of the methodology that iconic memory may store very large volume of information, for a very short time though.

Efficient methodology 488714 318617 – a procedure, for which a testee gets a task to make some complex of practical actions, through the character of which the conclusion on features of his psychology is to be made.

Method of addition 428614 319 81718 – group of methods, related to projective methods. They are: incomplete sentences and stories, associative tests of Carl Jung.

Method of research of products of creation 491 818 81789 – group of methods, belonged to projective method. They are test of human figure picture, picture of a Coch tree, picture of a house, drawing by a finger etc.

Methodology of expression study 498614 818 9 – group of methods, belonged to projective ones. They are handwriting and speech communication peculiarities analysis, Mira I Lopez myokinetic technique.

Methodology of interpretation 498619 3197 – group of methods, belonged to projective ones. They are Thematic Apperception Test (TAT), Rosenzweig picture-frustration test and Szondi test.

Methodology of catharsis 519 617 319 8198 – group of methods belongs to projective ones. They are: psychodrama, projective game.

Qualitative methodology 498612 718 19 – methods, based on the qualitative analysis of experimental data, and the tested quality is described in terms of known scientific notions. It does not allow applying of measures and methods of quantitative processing of results, to judge about the level of development of diagnosis features and to show directly the causal links among researched variables.

Quantitative methodology 519617 3194 5 – methods, based on the quantitative analysis of experimental data. It allows usage of quantitative measures and methods of quantitative processing of results, to esteem a diagnostic feature to the extent of its development relatively to other people.

Methodology of construction 519614 819 1 – group of methods belongs to projective method. They are: MAPS, test of the world and its modifications.

Mira-i-Lopez myokinetic method 498 617 8980 1948719 - one of the projective techniques relevant to the a group of methods of expression research.

Multi measures methodology 519614319 818 – the methodology, characterized by the fact that it is devoted to diagnostics and estimation of some similar or different psychological features at once.

Mono measures methodology 89742198 – methods, characterized by diagnosis or estimation of one quality or a feature.

Objective methodology 891871 808916 – methods, used the factors independent from consciousness or desires of a testee or an experimenter. The examples are the tests, included analysis of psychological or reflective indices or testee activity practical results, subjectivity of values for which is minimal.

Objective manipulation methodology 988 614071 21931 – methods, tasks of which solving by a testee, are proposed in the form of real things, with which one must do something: to collect out of given material, to make, to dismantle and etc.

Questionnaire methodology 9188 701418317 – methods, when a testee is asked questions orally and his answers are fixed and processed.

Peterson methodology 912816318 714 – a procedure for the definition of influence of the time of storage of information on the duration and quality of memorizing in the absence of repetition opportunity. The point is that after presentation a material which must be memorized, a testee is proposed to solve additional task during some time, which prevents the repetition of already memorized material.

Productive methodology 8901 617 488 – methods,

using a type of own creative production of a testee included verbal, imaginative, material spontaneously created or reproduced according to the instruction.

Projective methodology 814 319 818 – it has significant possibilities for research of personal individuality, and allows of indirect modeling of some life situations and relations to study personal formation, acting directly or by means of different mindsets, such as 'significant feelings', 'personal meaning' etc., for which the passion of personal reflection is displayed also.

Psychodiagnostic methodology 8901 617 917 318 – used to put psychological diagnosis. They are: blank method, objective-manipulation, projective, pictorial methods.

Picture methodology 489 061 719 317809 – methods of using of pictures of thematic or voluntary character created by a testee. Sometimes it is used the method of interpretation by a testee of just ready, standard pictures.

Sensory methodology 914 788901 909 – the method, presenting a test material in the form of physical stimuli, turned to sensory organs.

Conscious methodology 898 31489101 - methods, turned to consciousness of a testee. Their advantage is that they allow to judge of psychology of a testee directly – on the base that he or his partner speaks to him.

Methodology conjugated-motorial 498016 316 481 – the way of study of affective reactions of a man. In difference from the method of registration of symptoms of affective reactions through the change of vegetative functions (breathing, blood pressure, pulse etc.) allow to study the reflection of these reactions in speech and motorial processes.

Sociometric method 489612 8906 819 – in its base – the principle of choice of a partner for joint actions. A person, chosen by the most number of a group members, has a high range; one who is selected by no one- low status. But this methodology not allow to clear out the reasons and content of these or those relations, their motivational nucleus.

Method of dual stimulation 891016 3194 – the

methodology for a study of the process of formation of notions. There are 2 sets of stimuli in it, from which the 1st acts the function of an object, to which the activity of a testee is directed, and the 2nd — the function of signs, through which this activity is formed.

Method of structuring 51948 719 81 — a group of methods, belong to projective method. They are: test of spots by Rorschach, test of clouds, test of 3 dimension projection.

Subjective method 319617 819 48 — the method, using data, dependent from desires and consciousness of a testee or experimentalist — related to their inner experience and dependent on it. Classic example — introspective method, based on conclusions.

Technical method 518617 918489 — the method, giving a testee the test material in the form of records, videos, films, or through other technical devices.

Asserting method 318915 614 081 — the method, proposing some statements or assertions towards which a testee must agree or disagree.

Psychological method 489614 319 018 — the method, where a diagnostics is performed on the base of the analysis of involuntary physical or physiological reaction of an organism of a testee.

Methodology 489618 31914 — 1.Study of scientific method of research, widely it is method of cognition in general. 2. Complex of methods, used in a science. The system of principles and ways of organization and construction of theoretical and practical activity. It is embodied in organization and regulation of all sorts of human activity. In whole the methodology defines a principle, by which a man must be guided when proceeding activity.

Methodology applied-scientific 97618 31914 819 — working out of the same problems as the general scientific method does, but in frames of an applied science, with a view to features of an object of a science in relation to theory and empiric activity. It is performed in frames of the system of knowledge, created by schools of sciences differed with their explanatory principles and method of researches and practice..

General scientific methodology 489617 31948 – there are attempts of working out of universal principles, means and forms of scientific cognition, correlating (potentially) not with some separate science, but applied to wide circle of sciences, differed from philosophic method, to leave in frames of scientific cognition, not spreading to general worldview level. There are conceptions of the system of scientific analysis, structural-level approach, cybernetic principles of description of complex system etc. At this level general problems of construction of scientific study are worked out, in particular the ways of experiments forming-up, of observations and patterning.

Defense mechanism 519318 914 913 – associated with ego automatic unconscious mechanisms, providing psychic defense of a person. They are sublimation, substitution, ousting, regression, projection, rationalization, reactive formation, identification and fixation of behavior.

Mechanism of identification 489614 718 8918 – provides an indirect transfer of 'personal experience' through personal example, transfusion, imitation and etc.

Unconscious mechanism 519 614319 810 – there are subclasses: 1. unconscious automatics, 2. unconscious purposes, 3. unconscious accompanying of conscious actions.

Mechanism of mastering of a role 319618 719 801 (mechanism of acceptance and mastering of social roles) – it is similar to the mechanism of identification, differs though by more significant generalization and often by absence of personalization of acquiring model. It is described with the help of the notion of social position and social role.

Mechanism of transformation of a purpose– 489617 019 317 (transformation of an aim to a motive) – the same as the mechanism of motive's shift.

Starting inborn mechanism 489061 718 8194 – for the instinctive behavior can be expressed, it needs not only outer stimulating situation, but certain internal factors in form of necessities or motivations. As the result of such combination the impression is created that an animal reacts on some situation specifically in a certain moment. Such correlation between the type of an irritant and a type of reaction suggested an existence of some mechanism able to determine what namely form of behavior inherent to an animal ought to start in a certain case. This mechanism, inherent to the given specie and inbuilt in brain, got the name of starting inborn mechanism. It is considered that such mechanism in most cases controls the behavior of many species.

Mechanism of the shift of a motive 519 584 318 2188 (mechanism of aim's displacement by motive; transformation of an aim to a motive) – mechanism of formation of motives in the theory of activity. Its main point is that an aim, stimulated earlier for realization by a motive, acquires a self-stimulating power and becomes the motive over time. The process of the shift of a motive is subject to the general rule that object, idea, aim, which was long and constantly enriching with positive emotion, transforms into an independent motive. So the shift of a motive to aim occurs, in other words, the aim acquires the status of a motive. Such mechanism acts at all stages of personal development but in time those main motives of communication are changed, which enriches actions with positive emotions.

Dream (reverie) 489614 319 8 – the necessary condition of transformation of a reality, stimulating reason, motive of activity, complete finish of which is delayed; special form of imagination, located in a distant future and adjoining of high quality life images. Plans for future, expressed as subject's imagination and satisfying of needs and interests important for him/her.

Dreaming 917 481 81931 –special internal activities, in the form which is often wrapped up the imagination; is to create a mental image of a desired future

Mysophobia 489016 319 78 – a type of neurosis

characterized by pathological fear of pollution.

Micropsia 319317 918 49 – subjective decrease of visible dimension of distant objects. It may be determined by a damage of some parts of visual analyzer.

Micro social group 219 487 3194 – the nearest social environment of a man such as his family, friends, colleges, neighbors.

Mime 819417 919 321 – complex of movements of parts of a body, expressing the subject's state or his relation to environment. Specific mime is inherent to the higher animals too.

Myogram 489317 3194 - recording of the electrical activity of the skeletal muscles, made by a special device i.e. myograph (electro myograph).

Myography 519617 319 471214 – the method of research of a functional state of muscles through a registration of their potentials.

World personal 49514 894181987 31948 – completely subjective system of opinions, believes, ideas, desires and needs of an individual, which orient his behavior in outer world and define his perception. It is a constant configuration of active reactions and special attitudes which overrun all life situations and makes unique all perception and behavior of individual.

World outlook (view) – 594317 81498 – systems of outlook on objective world and a place of a man in it, on human's relation to the environment and to himself, and also determined by these views general life positions of people, their ideals, principles of cognition and activity, valuable orientations. As a subject of the worldview the social group and a personality really act. Worldview is a nucleus of social and individual consciousness. It is the reflection, common world understanding of a man, society and valuable attitude to them, defining social-political, philosophic, atheistic or religious, moral, esthetic and scientific-theoretical orientation of a man.

Myth 59861731914 – appearing on early stages of

history, specific form of a worldview, expressed as tales and stories. Myth is the step, through which an individual comes out from mass psychology.

Mnemonics 9186173148 – the system of various procedures, making easy the memorizing and increasing of memory volume through the formation of additional associations.

Mnemotechnics 591867 3914 – the system of special methods serving for the relief of memorizing. Essence of mnemotechnic approaches is the fact that retained information is structured and comprehended in some way.

Public opinion (social mind) 59867181948 – expressed as the form of certain views, ideas and presentations, the attitude of a social group to phenomena and problems of social life, touching common interests. It appears as the product of recognition of actual social problems, requiring the solving, and expressed as comparison or even disagreement of different views and positions towards a discussed question in approval, support or rejection, accusation of actions or lines of behavior.

Modality 59867181914 89 – one of the main feature of experiences, their qualitative characteristic; color for vision; tone and timber for hearing; smell for the smelling. Modal features of sensations distinguished from other features (spatial, temporal, intensity) reflect features of reality in the special coded form (the length of the light wave is recognized as the color, the frequency of sound waves is tone, etc.).

Modeling 319 488 5194 – in terms of psychology a study of a process and psyche states through their real (physical) or ideal mostly mathematical models. The system of objects and signs, reproducing some essential features of the system-original is considered as a model.

Psychological modeling 59867126801 – 1. Construction of some psychological processes running models for the purposes of formal control of their productiveness. 2. Recreation of psychic activity under the laboratory conditions for a study of its structure. It is performed by giving to a testee of various means which can be included in the structure of activity. As such means various trainings, schemes, maps, videos are used.

Model 58867191814 – a scheme, a picture or description of a natural or social, natural or artificial process, phenomena or an object.

Informational model 48871631918 – in ergonomics organized by the certain rules the collection of information about the object of control, technical device itself and outer environment. They are necessary in situations, when an operator needs to evaluate the way of activity being supported rather by properties, measurable by instrumental ways than by observed features of components of ergatic system.

Conceptual model 598642 31914 80 – the notion, used in engineering psychology. Means the system of opinions of a man-operator about aims of his activity, state of an object of control and ways of influence on it.

Image-conceptual model 519 64891814 –Integrity of operator's views about real and anticipated state of an object of activity and erratic system in the whole as well as about aims and ways of realization of his activity.

Model / filtration 4986173191418 (model with filtration) – one of the first conceptions of selective attention. It supposes limitation of capacity of the system of processing of sensory information, going in parallel through some canals. At this certain stage of processing a signal occurs to be in the center of attention, that causes its transfer through selective filter of the canal with limited capacity. Due to the filter the transition of information from the short-time into the long-time memory takes place.

Modification 2198163181901 – type change, transformation of something, usually characterized by appearance of new features.

Modification of behavior 59867131919 – proposed by American psychologists-behaviorists method of regulation of social behavior. It was used as the first clinic method of psychotherapy for treatment of neurosis; it was used further for mentally healthy people for working out of mechanical habits, providing adaptation to unacceptable for them life conditions.

Brain 314 218 318 818 – the central part of man's and animal's nervous system, the main organ of psyche. Spinal cord and cerebrum are distinguished for vertebrate animals and human beings anatomically. Brain is covered by 3 coverings: hard, arachnoidal and vascular. The tissue of cerebrum consists of the grey (complex of nervous cells) and white (neuronal cells processes assembly of the brain) substances.

Brain: biorhythm 598614 81931 – one of the types of background, spontaneous electric activity of man's and animal's brain. Biorhythms are the regular or rhythmic activity, characterized by prolonged repetition of a wave as insignificantly modified by frequency of its repetition.

Cerebrum 814 729 318 818 – the part of nervous system included in the cranium and consists of great brain, cerebellum, pons varolii and medulla.

Cerebrum: cortex 918 617 619 017 – upper layer of cerebrum hemispheres consists of nervous cells of vertical orientation (pyramidal cells) and also of ascending and descending projection nerves. It is typical in the neuroanatomical context by presence of horizontal layers, which differ in length, width, density, form and dimention of constituent nervous cells.

Cerebrum: function: lateralization 498 614 719 816 – (brain cord functions lateralization) the process of redistribution of psychic functions between the left and right hemispheres of brain taken place at the stage of ontogenesis.

Brain ancient (reptile) 519 614 319 817 – the group of nervous structures forming the 'low stage' of human brain; which corresponds to the first stage of brain development in phylogenesis up to reptiles.

Medulla 214 713 914 819 – continuation of spinal cord in the cortex cavity.

Spinal cord 314 218 814 719 – divided into 4 parts; thorax, lumbar, cervical, and also into segments (31-33segments). The continuation of the spinal cord in the cortex cavity is the medulla.

Moment temporal 489317918 14 – temporal confusion of some processes of sexual development in child age, that was associated by S.Freud with early maturity.

Monospection 498 814 31941 – the general term for the definition of introspection and extrospection in certain sense as an observation of outer events, their registration, which at the same time is the registration of own experiences of observer as well as an observation for his/her own inner psychic states.

Monotony 819617 3194 – a functional state of a man appeared as monotonous activity. It is characterized by decrease of tonus and perception, reduction of conscious control, reduction of attention and loss of the interest for a work.

Monophobia 498617 918 48 – pathological fear of loneliness.

Morals (ethics) 549317 61914 – morality, the complex of norms and principles of individual behavior in the relation to society and other people i.e. one of the main forms of social consciousness.

Autonomous morality 528641 3184 – the rules, established by a man for himself which may be changed by him.

Morals heteronomy 528641 31817 –rules worked out by other people which are considered as obligatory and 'sacred' for given individual.

Moratorium 89161731814 – delay of performance of some duties. In psychology the term is understood widely metaphoric.

Psychic moratorium 49861731818 – the crisis period between the youth and adultness, during which the multidimensional complex processes of acquiring of an adult identity and new relation to the world occur in a personality.

© Grabovoi G.P., 2003

Morita therapy 319481 61914 – founded on the base of statements of Zen Buddhism through the use of psychological effects of sensory deprivation. Firstly it was oriented on the treatment of such ethnotypical Japanese disease as shinkeishitsu (neurotic complex with elements of neurasthenia, hypochondria and obsession). The main aim is a client achievement of not just good self-feeling, but the change of the life being.

Mortido 9189180418417 4184 – a drive to death as an aggressive drive of an energy, one of the most essential motives of psychic life.

Pons valorii 498 617 319 148 – the part of the central nervous system, lying above the medulla. It contains many centers, responsible for complex reflexes.

Motive 428 617 319 18 – 1. Stimuli for activity, associated with satisfaction of subject's needs; complex of outer or inner conditions, arising subject's activity and defining its direction. 2. An object, material or ideal, achievement of which is the reason of activity as stimulating and defining the choice of direction of the activity for the purpose of which it is performing. 3. Conscious reason laid at root of the choice of actions and personal behavior.

Leading motive 519 716 9919 – the main motive as courage for an activity in case of its multimotivated state.

Motive of power 591648 319181 – constant personal feature, expressing the need of a subject for possessing of the power over other people i.e. the striving to dominate, to control.

Motive of achievement 489617 31998 – the need to achieve a success in various activities, especially in situations of competition with others. Constant motivational feature of a personality, opposite to the motive of avoidance.

Avoidance motive 5986193191 – an inclination to act in such a way in any situation in order to avoid faults; especially if the results of activity are perceived and estimated by other people. Constant motivational personal feature, opposite to the achievement motive.

Unconscious motive 49861431971 – this motive is more than conscious one; up to the certain age practically all motives are unconscious. This is special activity, having own motive of self-cognition and moral self-development. Unconscious motives however show mentally, in special forms though. They are emotions and personal meanings in the very least.

Conscious motive 5219317 818 14 – (motive – target) – big life purposes, managing of an activity during the long period of life. These are motives- targets. Their existence is typical for mature personality.

Prosocial motive 41861731814 – the motive of behavior, containing an expressed and conscious striving to make good.

Motive- stimulus 498688 71918 – a secondary motives caused an activity in case of its multimotivated state. They rather stimulate this activity additionally than only 'start' it.

Motivation 48864131811 – there are stimuli, caused the activity of an organism and defining its direction. Conscious or unconscious psychic factors, promoting an individual for performance of certain actions and defining their direction and aims. In wide sense the term is used in all spheres of psychology studied the reasons and mechanisms of purposeful man and animal behavior.

Intrinsic motivation 42168171919 – promotes an individual for an action with the aim to improve his state of confidence and independence, contrary to external towards him purpose.

Achievement motivation 598614319 19 – one of types of the motivation of activity, associated with the need to achieve a success and avoid faults, the striving for a success in types of activity. In its base there are emotional experiences, associated with social acceptance of success, achieved by an individual.

Motivation 289174218 319 – the rational explanation by a subject of the reasons of activity through a pointing at

© Grabovoi G.P., 2003

the social acceptable for him and his reference group circumstances, boosted to choose the given action. It differs from actual motives of behavior and acts as one of the form of recognition of these motives.

Motility 598 611 819 318 – motion activity

Motility internal 598 611 918 688- a concept to describe the experience gained of human beings' programs for motor actions fulfillment in the past.

Courage 5986819 06888914 – a personal quality, expressed as ability to act decisively and purposefully under complex or dangerous conditions, to control impulses, to overcome possible fear and uncertainty, the ability to mobilize all forces for the achievement of an aim. Its highest display is heroism.

Thought (idea) 928 688 714316 – the basic unity, 'molecule' of thinking. In thoughts the process of world understanding, understanding of other people and himself is expresses. At the bottom of a thought there is a reflection of such fundamental features of phenomena as their similarity and cohesion in time and space etc.

Thinking 8 9888 418 704 319 – one of the highest psychic display, the process of cognitive activity of an individual, process of modeling of not-occasional relations of outer world, characterized by general and mediate reflection of reality: analysis and demands of solving task and ways of its solving. Discrete mental operations which thinking originates are formed in this constant process, but it is not identical to them. Thinking as a process is tightly associated with thinking as a personal activity with motivation abilities.

Thinking: syncretism 8418 704 31991 – a feature of logical development. Consciousness, expressed as classifying of objects and phenomena, defined by a notion, according to different, logically non-consequent or even incompatible features.

Thinking non-imaginative 8 704 319 814 617 – the notion, means the thinking free of sense elements of cognition i.e. images of perception, recepts and speech constructions.

Visual thinking 8 9888 418912 – the way of creative solving of a problem tasks in the context of imaginative modeling. The ground of visual thinking is outwardly active and outwardly imaginative thinking, when at assimilation of objective practical and sensuous practical actions with features of the objects, outer perceptive actions are formed.

Discursive thinking 8 18 704 319 316 – a form of thinking strategy, for which the successive search of different variants of a task solving is performed, often on the base of logically associated reasoning, when every next step is determined by results of previous ones. Often discursive thinking is opposed by the intuitive thinking.

Preoperative thinking 4319 894171 – a stage of development of the intellect of a child from 2 through 7 years. It is characterized by beginning of formation of symbolic function which allows to differ the defining from the defined; it acts as the ground of a layout of recept. Initially a child uses delayed imitation, game symbol, picture, mental image, speech construction in the capacity of the instrument of definition. Due to this he can mentally disconnect an object and construct it from parts.

Intuitive thinking 9888 418 4 319 289 – one of types of thinking. It *is* characterized by speed of behavior, absence of precisely expressed stages, little consciousness. Often it is opposed by the discursive thinking.

Complex thinking 8788 418 704 319 – the notion for the definition of a stage in development of child's concepts, located between syncretic and true notions. Organized complexes are characterized by empiric generalization on the base of perceivable relations among objects.

Thinking outwardly active 598 418 704 319 – one of types of thinking, characterized by the fact that task solving is performed through real, physical transformation of a situation, trials of objects features; form of a thought, included in real manipulation of objects and serves the practical tasks.

Outwardly imaginative thinking 8 418 704 319 – in its base there is a modeling and solving of a problem situation in the context of recepts. It is associated with recept of situations and transformations in them. All variety of different factorial features of objects are recreated especially full with its help, because the view of an object from some points of view may be fixed in an image.

Practical thinking 3219 918 614 788 – a type of thinking, usually compared with theoretical thinking, where a solving of a problems is realized in outer practical activity. Associated with aim, work out of plans and projects and often it is done in the lack of time, that sometimes makes it more difficult than theoretical thinking. In contradiction to theoretical thinking there is no task of processing of new methodological means, which may transfer in principally other situations.

Pralogical thinking 499 418 704 319 – a notion for characterizing of thinking of members of primitive societies, sort of principally opposed to logical thinking of modern people for the definition of early stage of thinking development, when the formation of its main logical laws were not built yet: the existence of causal-effect relations is recognized, but their essence serves in mystifying form. Phenomena correlates by the feature of cause-effect and when they just coincide in time.

Thinking verbal-logical 8 528 9888 418 704 – a type of thinking, characterized by use of notions, logical constructions. Functioning on the base of speech means and is the latest stage of historical and ontogenetic development of thinking. Different types of generalizations are formed and are functioning within.

Creative thinking 8 888 468 704 319 – a type of thinking, characterized by creation of subjectively new product during the cognitive activity towards its creation. These new formations concern the motivation, aims, values and senses.

Theoretical thinking 18 70 4 319 8 — a type of thinking, which is usually opposed to the practical thinking. It is directed to the reveal of laws, objects features.

μ rhythm 9181114 319 7 — biorhythm, fixed in the sphere of fissure of Rolando of cerebrum, changes of which are associated only with the influence of kinesthetic irritants. During the performance of any motions this rhythm is blocked. It is similar to alfa-rhythm by frequency and amplitude.

_H_

Observancy 289317 498611 — an ability, expressed as the ability to note essential, characterized by, even invisible features of objects and phenomena. It supposes curiosity and is to be acquired in life experience. Its development is the important task of formation of cognitive attitude and adequate perception of reality.

Observation 8916918 906 781 — 1. Research of the world at the level of emotional cognition, purposeful and conscious. Perception of a process with the aim to reveal its invariant features without active involvement in the process. Personal features of perception, attitudes, direction of a person are revealed in observation.

Systematic observation 898618 718 067 — at that attention must be concentrated on one certain act of behavior in order to precisely describe its features on which research is focused.

Standardized observation 498 681 719 4 — performed for scientific purposes the observation for people behavior according to the certain scheme of observation which reflects, what needs to be observed, in what way to perform observation and how to present its result.

Skill (habit) 989 061 719 41 — (automatic act, secondary automatism) — an act, formed through the repetition, characterized by high degree of acquirement and absence of successive conscious regulation and control.

Skill: formation: mechanism 512 618 718911 — during the formation of a skill there are many phases, united in more general periods. A primary introduction with a motion and primary mastering occur for the 1st period. 2. 2nd period is the period of automation of motion. There is full transfer of separate components of the motion or the whole motion under the control of background levels.

Motor skill 488 718 499016 – automatic influence on the outer object through motions for the purposes of its transformation, performed many times before.

Intellectual skill 4890 16 319 14 – automatic technique, the way of solving of the repeatedly presented mental task.

Perceptual skill 899 716 30917 – automatic emotional reflections of features and qualities of well known, perceived before object.

Obsession 988061 78806 – the characteristic of phenomena and psychic processes, means uncontrollable for consciousness ones, their performance in spite of a desire, often in spite of a subject. Obsession as a psychological phenomenon expresses various forms.

Hope (promise) 489061 719 88 0618 – an emotional experience, arising in expectation by a subject of some desirable event, reflects an anticipated possibility of its real realization. It is formed as the result of cognition of reasons, conditioning of expected events, or on the base of subjective emotional experience, cumulated in similar situations in the past. Foreseeing the possible development of events, a hope plays the role of inner regulator of an activity and helps the subject to define its effects.

Reliability 3178 719 88 0618 – one of the most important features of methods and tests; one of the criteria of their quality, related to precision of psychological measurement. It reflects the precision of psychological measuring and stability of the result towards an action of outer factors. The higher the validity of tests or methods the more they are free from errors of measuring.

Superconscious 891614 318 911 – being not subject to an individual consciousness and volitional control, the level of psychic activity of a personality in solving of creative tasks.

Intention 519314 819 4 – conscious striving to complete action according to the planned program, aimed at achievement of a supposed result.

Psychic tension 591 419 – a psychic state, determined by anticipation of unprofitable development of an event. It is accompanied by the sense of general discomfort and fear. In difference with a fear, it includes the readiness to control the situation, to act on it in a certain way.

Narcoanalysis 489 316 71 – therapy branch, method and procedure of modified psychoanalysis performed against a background of the drug action enabling the operational establishment of a transfer and overcoming of a client's resistance; so it provides intensification and increase of effectiveness of psychoanalytical interview and treatment.

Narcomania (drug addiction) 518 712618 44 – a pathological drive to drug addiction; a disease, arising as the result of drug addiction, caused euphoria in a little dose and narcotics dream in large ones. It shows irresistible drive to use drugs, caused by a habit, appearing when systematic using of drugs; tendency to increase dozes, formation of the abstinent syndrome.

Disorder of attention 498 611 01931 – a painful disorder, to various extent it is observed as exhaustion and organic damages of brain of frontal lobes mostly. It shows inadequate changes of direction and selectivity of an activity and coordination of separate actions. It may appear as the narrowing of the range of attention, its instability and distraction to lateral irritants.

Personality disorder 519361 819 41 – system disorders of behavior socially typical for various psychic diseases and local damages of brain.

Thinking disorder 599 788 319 418 – disorders towards performance of intellectual operations conditioned upon different psychic diseases, local damages of brain and anomaly of psychic development.

Sensory defect 596 714918 41 – deafness, blindness.

Sensory distance disorder 596 714918 48 – weak vision of objects at a distance out of limits of physical vision or in other time interval.

Disorder phantom 489317 918 4 – false senses such as pain, anemia, convulsion etc. from the non-existent part of a body after amputation. It may have obsessive heavy character.

Narcissism 988 061 319 48 – a state and direction of libido to ego. Normal stage of sexual development. One of the distinguishing features of neurosis is the delay at this stage of psychosexual development.

Narcissism: stroke 8061 319 48 91 – (3 strokes on human narcissism). In the process of development of science there were 3 strokes on human pride: 1. cosmologic stroke by Copernicus 2. biological stroke of Darwin 3. psychological stroke to be the most sensitive by psychoanalytical theory, proved indisputable dominance of unconscious over consciousness and leading role of unconscious spiritual processes towards organization of life activity and behavior.

Secondary narcissism 8 061 319 48 – the term means the phenomenon of secondary narcissism, appearing as the result of orientation from libido to ego. It is interpreted as passion directed to ego as the result of identification.

Violence compensatory 498 688 319 4 – violence serving for an impotent, deprived in a private capacity person as a substitute of productive activity and a way to get a revenge against life.

Reactive violence 598611 819 48 – violence, expressed as defense of life, freedom, dignity or possessions. This form of violence 'serves the life' and has its aim as preservation.

Delight (pleasure) 519411 819 14 – one of the positive spiritual senses, associated with decrease, reduction or fading of quantity of irritants for a soul.

Final delight 519411 819 148 – final satisfaction from sexual activity, accompanied by sexual secretions.

Coprophilous delight 819 317 918 14 – delights of childhood, associated with defecation.

Anticipatory pleasure 719411 819 181 – enjoyment from stimulation of erogenic zones, preceding a sexual act.

Persistence 498114 319 8 – a personal volitional quality, characterized by ability to overcome outer and inner obstacles aimed at indeclinable, in spite of difficulties and obstacles, achievement of an aim realization.

Mood 898 716 31944 – comparatively long constant psychic states of moderate or weak intensity expressed as positive or negative emotional background of psychic life of a person. It is characterized by diffusion, absence of precisely conscious touch to certain objects or processes, stability allowing to consider the mood as a separate factor of a temperament.

Public mood (public sentiment) 598 716 31944 – dominant state of senses and minds of social groups in a certain period of time. Not only mass phenomena of social psychology, but one of the most significant forces, promoting people to an activity, reflecting on behavior of different groups and social layers, also classes, nations and even commonweal. It is expressed in all areas of social life activity.

Operative adjustment 598411 69814 – preparation for performance of an action under the given conditions, according to which the precision, tempo, tension, stability, duration, way and style of further activity are established. During the operational adjustment the preparation of neurodynamic system of an organism occurs.

Science 528 716 319 81 – a sphere of activity, the main function of which is the working out of knowledge of the world, its systematization on the ground of which it is possible to construct the image of the world i.e. scientific world view and ways of interaction with world as scientifically grounded practice.

Science: classification 716 319 81 88 9 – the word 'science' denotes as well separate branches of scientific knowledge, which consequently differ by a set of essential features. First of all fundamentals are distinguished by their object (an object of science differs from a thing of science). The main scientific objects are: nature (organic and not organic), a man (society and thinking). So, there are natural sciences and the humanitarian area of science; the last is subdivided into social and philosophic ones. So, there are 3 main parts of scientific knowledge or 3 complexes of sciences. Besides these 3 main parts there are large divisions at the junction of the main branches. There are possible other ways of differentiation of sciences. So, it is acceptable the division on fundamental and applied sciences. Under all these schemes psychology takes its place. The joint of psychology and natural sciences is obvious especially for biology. For scientific psychology it is characteristic borrowings of some biological theoretical statements for grounding of regularities of psychic development.

Science: object 528 716 31819 88 – the facet of reality, the given science is directed to the study of which. Often an object is fixed on the name of a science. But while no science is capable to describe its object completely, it ought to limit the sphere of its own interest rejecting from study of some aspects of the object.

Science: rational approach 8 716 319 819 – comes at least to Plato; later bright representatives are Descartes, Kant, Hegel. It supposes that any true knowledge may originate from an intellect only, and only the intellect must play the main role in explanation of facts either in ontological context or relatively to cognition or action. The best way to formulate a certain problem and try to find out an answer consists in a search of logical arguments. As the result, it was discussed for many centuries what it might be, instead of to observe the existing in reality.

Science: empirical approach 5928 7176 3149 881 – it lain down on the base of experimentation. It makes the main focus on experience and so radically differs from rational approach.

Science: thing 5328 716 3919 881 – facets, by which

the object of a science is presented there. If an object exists independently for a science, the thing is formed together with it and fixed by its notional system. The thing does not fix all sides of an object, though may include what is absent in the frames of an object. In certain sense development of science is the development of its thing.

Humanitarian area of science 716 3179 81 – its object is a man, human society, and thinking. The humanities are divided into social and philosophic sciences.

Natural science 91528 716 319 81 – its object is nature, organic and not organic.

Applied science 428 716 319 81 518 – they are sciences, oriented on practical application of knowledge. They are received from fundamental sciences; they serve the needs of a society.

Fundamental science 8529 716 319 81989 – (pure science) – they are sciences, researching the world independently from a possibility of practical use of received knowledge.

Learning 847136 3919 512 – a process and a result of acquiring of an individual experience.

Verbal learning 7136 39129 5192 – learning through verbal influences: instruction, explanation, description etc. without addressing to concrete objective actions, to operational or conditional and reflective stipulating.

Vicarious learning 936 39819 512 – learning through direct observation towards emotionally presented images and through imitation of them.

Operant learning 498614 318 12 – a type of learning, going due to spontaneous the subject's derivations of a lot of various reactions on one and the same situation or stimulus with further fixation of those only which are the most successful concerning the obtained result.

Social learning 3919 512 498611 – the term means an organism acquiring of new form of reaction through the observation of the others' behavior and its imitation.

Conditional-reflective learning 747136 918 417 41 –

a type of learning, occurs due to the processing of reactions on new irritants according to the mechanism of conditional reflex.

Neurasthenia (neurataxia) 4815421181 – one of the types of neurosis, which may be shown as the result of overexhaustion or infections (for children).

Neurosis 48154211 – a group of the most spread borderline neuropsychic disorders, psychogenic by nature, but not conditioned upon psychotic state. It appears on the base of not productive, irrationally solved neurotic conflict, rooted mainly in childhood, under conditions of damaged relations to micro social environment e.g. to parents.

Neurosis: reason 948154211 – appears where the transition from direct to inhibited towards an aim sexual primary urge was not successful properly; it corresponds to the conflict between primary calls, immersed ego, which underwent such a development and parts of these calls, which strive for direct satisfaction out of substitute unconscious sphere. The reason of neurosis appears as the joint of two main components: 1.inherited predispositions due to fixation of libido as the result of inherited sexual constitution and associated with it prehistoric and infant feelings; 2. accidental traumatic experience.

Neurosis: remission spontaneous 4815421108 – (spontaneous remission of neurosis) a process of self induced, mainly from internal reason reduction and weakening of painful displays of neurosis.

Actual neurosis 4815421129 – a group of disorders, expressed as immediate somatic sequences of sexual damages.

Neurosis great 481542116 – the most spread and significant forms of modern neurosis: 1. Neurotic affectionateness as search for love and approval whatever it takes. 2. Neurosis of power i.e. the chase for power, prestige and possession 3. Neurosis of submissiveness as automated conformism 4. Neural isolation or escape from a society.

Hysterical neurosis 548154211 – a form of neurosis, characterized by different clinic symptoms. It is often expressed by convulsions, astasia–abasia, hysterical deafness, blindness, mutism and vegetative visceral disorders. It is especially characterized by such features as shallowness, demonstrativeness, and situational differentiation. Enuresis and anorexia are typical for hysteric children.

Neurosis clinical 481 54 21 191 – one of the main form of neuropsychic disorders. The reason is so called neurotic conflict, activating in psycho-traumatic situations. Organic changes of brain are often absent. There are 3 forms of clinic neurosis: neurasthenia, hysteria and obsessive neurosis.

Neurosis of obsessive 4815421148 – one of the types of neurosis, the possibility of its appearance is large for people with rigid, suspicious character. Besides general neurotic symptoms it is expressed by high anxiety and suppressed mood, obsessive thoughts of different content, recalls, actions and also phobias (cardiophobia, cancerophobia, fear of blushing) experienced as alien and forcibly repeated.

Neurosis collective obsessive 481542113 – religions are its form.

Narcissistic neurosis 148154211 – their feature is the fixation of libido on early phases, preceding the phases of hysteria or obsessive neurosis and its direction to ego, increasing the level of ambivalence senses. Typical feature is active participation of ego in the origin of diseases and their correlation to the conflict between ego and Superego.

Noogenic neurosis 64815421 – the neurosis originated from loss of the reason to live.

Transference neurosis of 5481542119 – the general denotation of 3 forms of neurosis: hysteria of fear, conversion hysteria and obsessive neurosis. The origin is considered to be the conflict and fight of sexual drives with preservation instincts, between demands of sexuality and ego or between Ego and It. This is typical attempts of ego defense against sexuality and in this context there is a result of conflict between ego and libido attachment to an object.

This neurosis is the subject of psychoanalysis.

Neurosis of fear (anxiety) 6848154211 – a form of neurosis, which was developed as a response to the psychic traumas and the main symptom is free fear (anxiety syndrome). At that the phobia either is not located or associated with certain organ of a body or concrete situation (phobia of height, of enclosures). The common reason is frustrated excitement; libido excitement is caused but not satisfied, and the unsatisfied libido transforms into a phobia.

Traumatic (accident) neurosis 4815421171 – a disease, coming as the result of mechanical impacts, mechanical trauma. In certain circumstances ego is interested in the appearance and existence of such neurosis, as profitable form of defense from a danger.

Universal neurosis 48 154 21161 – general 'collective' neurosis with various functions. It may be a religion effectively defended from a danger of personal neurosis.

Experimental neurosis 3148 154211 – arising for animals under special conditions of physiological experiment the state, characterized by a damage of adaptive behavior, inability to process new and not working of old conditional reflexes, rejection from food, vegetative disorders and damage of a dream. Being the model of clinic neurosis of a person, it is used for the study of the mechanism of nervous system activity.

Neuroticism 598 154211 – a state, characterized by emotional instability, anxiety, low self-respect and vegetative disorders. It ought not to identify as neurosis for the neurotic symptoms may be observed for a healthy man. It is usually measured through special scales or personal questionnaire.

Neurotic 54811 319 4 – a man under influence of neurosis i.e. repressed personality, bad adaptable to outer world; dominant behavior is emotional-instinctive reactions. It is explained by the domination of the principle of satisfaction over the principle of reality. Neurotic is a man who is in the road of himself/herself.

Neurotic: sexual drive 64811 319 48 – characterized

by presence of different variations of normal sexual life and expression of painful forms.

Negativism (negation) 519 448 9184 – not-motivational behavior, expressed as actions, opposite to claims and desires of other persons of a social group. Refusal to be under influence of other people, caused not by logics of the performance of own tasks, but negative attitude to them. It is conditioned upon the action of psychological defense in response to affects, contradicted to inner senses of a subject.

Child negation 448 918479 – a form of child communication, when he/she tries to defend the rights of his/her personality trough contradictions to claims of other people. It may be expressed as stubbornness, cruelty, closeness.

Independence 598 511 – an alternative to conformity and negation e.g. self-processing and defense of own position. It not excludes the solidarity of a person with a group, but not by pressure, but on the ground of conscious agreement with it.

Neurolinguistics 564317 90961 – a branch of a science, boundary for psychology, neurology and linguistics, studies brain mechanisms of speech activity when changing of speech processes, appearing as local disorders of brain.

Neuron 814 317 914 917 – a nerve cell with all its organs, dendrites and long sprout i.e. axon, also ending apparatus of synapses. The main function of the neuron is irritation, spread through an axon as short-time electric nervous signals and impulses.

Neuron-detector 814 317 914 919 – a nerve cell, selectively reacting to certain sensory features of complex irritant.

Neuropsychism 891491 614 – the theory in natural science, according to which only creatures with nervous system have psyche.

Neuropsychology 489 314 818 71 – a branch in a science, formed at the intersection of psychology, medicine and physiology. It studies brain mechanisms of the highest psychic functions following the material of local damages of brain. It considers the correlation of brain and psyche.

Neurophysiology 519 31791814 714 – a part of physiology devoted to the study of nervous system through electro-physiological methods.

Non-congruence 498617 31914 – non-correspondence of man's experiences and his recepts of himself/herself. It means anxiety, sensitivity and wholeness of a personality at the level of manifestations.

Necrophile 918 616 0496 – a personality and a type of personality, oriented on love for dead, destruction and death. The contrary notion is biophile.

Necrophilia 0496 411 06 – 1. sexual perversion, expressed as the drive and desire to possess a dead body; 2. Asexual painful striving to be near corps, to contemplate, to manipulate and decompose them.

Hatred (hate) 498 681 019 4 – constant active negative subject's sense, directed to phenomena, contradicting his needs, values, assertions. Able to call not only self-evaluation of own object, but active activity, aimed against it.

Neo - behaviorism 319 688 71 9 – a concept of American psychology, appeared in 30[ies] years of XX c. It accepted the main postulate of behaviorism that the object of psychology is objectively contemplated reactions of an organism to outer stimuli, neobehaviorism filled it by the notion of changeable mediums as the factors, which serve a medical chain between influence of stimuli and backward muscle motions. Following the methodology of operationalism, adherents of neobehaviorism considered that the content of the notion of 'changeable mediums' meant 'unobserved' cognitive and motivational components of behavior, is perhaps to be found out experimentally through the use of features, defined by researchers' operations.

Neo-psychoanalysis 598 617 31 9 1 – 1. Concept in terms of psychology, psychoanalysis and psychotherapy, oriented on the synthesis of different spheres of psychoanalysis at the aim of complex explanation of neurosis, e.g. dynamic interaction of a drive and ousting, also at the aim of modern therapy. 2. Sometimes the notion is used for general denotation of various new trends in psychoanalysis, mainly oriented on the study of therapeutic aspects.

Neophobia 498 617 31 – pathological fear of all new or non-habitual.

Neofreudism 591688 41 – a direction in modern philosophy, sociology, psychology and psychoanalysis, developed from freudism, adherents of which try to overcome the biologism of classic freudism and lead its basic statements into social context.

Nystagmus 519 317 48 – rhythmic movement of an eye's apple. It consists of slow motion in some direction and fast return.

Newborn-ness 489712 618418 – a period the age from the birth to 4-6 weeks when the primary adaptation of a child to outer world occurs.

Nosophobia 481542198 – a type of neurosis, characterized by pathological fear of diseases.

Non-conformism 319 316 418 - a striving to contradict the opinion of the majority and to act in the opposite way. The synonym is negation.

Norm 519 514 12 – established measure, an average value of something.

Group norm 519 514 1298 – complex of rules and demands, processing of each really acting society; the important mean of regulation of their interaction, interactivity and communication.

Social norm 5819 514 12 – accepted in a concrete society or a group the rules of behavior, regulating people interrelations.

Test norm 519 514 98 – average estimation for the given test of large group of normal healthy people of certain age and culture, factors with which it is possible to compare the marks of a testee, evaluating his level and making conclusions of weather they are higher or lower than the norm. Test norm is the middle level of development of large collective of people similar to a testee towards a set of social-demography characteristics.

Normalization 48519 514 12 – 1. Establishment of a norm, model. 2. Regulation, normalization. 3. The same as standardization.

Group normalization 481519 514 12 – social-psychological phenomenon, appearing as the result of group discussion, when primary different and even extreme positions of members are smoothed and opinion of mutual average character is acquired.

Morals (ethics) 498104817 9181 – regulating function of human behavior. Its essence is concluded in elimination of drives.

_O_

Generalization 498614 312 – the product of mental activity, the reflection form of reality phenomena common features and qualities. Cognitive process, leading to singling out and denotation of approximately constant features of outer world. The simplest forms of generalization are realized already at the level of perception, as the stability of perception. Its types correspond to types of thinking. Generalization also acts as the mean of human activity. At the level of human thinking it is mediated through the use of society processed tools like ways of cognitive activity and signs.

Theoretical generalization 498614 3189 – based on the extraction of significant ties among phenomena of outer world, witnessed of their genetic similarity. It is supported by hidden important features, coming out of frames of immediate observation principles i.e. hypothesis. It is realized through notions, where only most significant is fixed and particulars are omitted. The ability for theoretical generalization is formed especially intensive at teen age and in young days.

Empiric generalization 498614 318 – compilation based on the immediately observed or experienced features of objects and phenomena. Use such features as classifying gives a man possibility to work with larger volume of things than it is possible in perceptual context. Every new object is recognized as related to a certain class through classifying schemes.

Smell (osphoresis, osmesis) 519 418 3194 –an ability to scent substances as to smell. Chemical substances, spread as vapor, gas, dust etc., come into nose cavity, where they interact with corresponding receptors. Besides chemoreceptors, some other receptors may take part in the formation of senses of smell, the receptors of mucous membrane of oral cavity: tactile, pain, temperature. So, some smelling substances call only make smell senses (vanilla, valeriana), other act in a package (menthol gives sense of cold, chloroform brings a sweetness).

Secondary processing 498 801614 7148 – a repeated process of dream change, beginning after the dream stands in front of consciousness as an object of perception.

Image 319418 418 – a subjective world view or its fragments, subjective presenting of external world things determined by either emotionally perceivable features or hypothetical constructs. It incorporates a subject itself, other people, spatial surrounding and temporal succession of events.

Perceptual image 43194818 41898 – a reflection in subjective aspect of real objects and their qualities with which an active subject interacts.

Hypnagogic image 965319418 4818 – appears as dreams and day-dream states.

Whole world image 591498 617 – multi-level system of human presentations of the world, of other people, of him/her self and activity of his/her own. The idea of wholeness and succession when originating, development and functioning of cognitive sphere of a personality is embodied.

Operational image 899418 418 – the reflection of subject's consciousness of such object or phenomenon, at which the action is aimed. The completeness of operational image is strictly defined by the necessity of adequate performance of the action, so, all excessive features of the object do not compose it. Due to this its laconic type and reliability is achieved, what is necessary for successful performance of the task under common or difficult conditions.

Global operational image 319418894 18 – an operational image, serves the base for performance of the whole action. It mainly includes the features of the final state of an object of action.

Operational stage image 319417 994 18 – an operational image, serves the base for evaluation of current states of actions with an object: recognition of signals, comparison of the current object's state with the given one.

After-image 9319418 41488 - visual senses, perceived during some, usually not long time, after finishing the action of an optical irritant.

Phantom image 53119418 418 – illusive senses at amputated part of a body. It is characterized by obsessive senses of pain, anemia etc., subjectively located at the absent part of a body.

Eidetic image 93194718 418 – subjective images of objects or object compositions distinctive and detailed for some time preserved after the finish of their actual perception. What is distinguished from after-images they are independent of eyes movements and relatively stable at a time. It often occurs in regard to a child of pre-school and teen age and rather seldom to adults.

Education 598614 3191 – 1. Learning, complex of knowledge, received in the course of special education 2. Anything, performed from something.

Reactive education 5918614 3191491 – one of the defensive mechanisms e.g. the form of psychological defense, characterized by change of unacceptable for conscious tendency or a way of behavior to opposite; directly opposite for an unacceptable towards ego situations' substitution.

Obsession 918 422 519 4 – a variant of obsessive

states, revealed in the course of experiences and actions and not required the certain situation for their appearance (obsessive hand-washing, fear of the number 3, fear to step on a line etc.)

Conditioning 319 418 5191 – formation of conditional reflexes.

Operant conditioning 4319 4188 5191 – a term means the special way of formation of conditional ties. So at the beginning an animal produces an action (spontaneous or stimulated by an experimenter) and then get a support.

Trainability (teachability) 398117 918 – individual marks of speed and quality of acquirement of knowledge and skill of a man during education.

Teaching 319 314 8917 918 – a process of purposeful transfer (organization) of knowledge and skills.

Latent learning 314 8998417 918 – a formation of certain skills in situations, when their direct use is not necessary and they are become not required. It is based on the formation for a subject of an image of whole situation and his/her action on it as the result of approximate research activity of a subject.

Learning obligatory 14 89 91817 918 – a lot of instinctive actions must pass the period of establishment and training during an individual development of an animal. Such form has got the name of obligatory learning (bird's flight, singing).

Problem teaching 8917 918 819 – a system of methods and means of education, which base is the modeling of real creative processes due to the creation of problem situations and control of a search of the problem solving.

Programmed teaching 419 314 8917 617 – a system of methods and means of education, which base is the self (independent) acquiring of knowledge and skills by pupils due to the step-by-step mastering of a material.

Training (simulator) teaching 519 314 84917 917 – an education, built on the principle of imitation of real technological process or an action of technical devices.

Facultative teaching 314 8917 918 9 – a process of mastering of new, specific individual form of behavior. It provides more plasticity in comparison with obligate teaching.

School education: psychological preparedness 51319 314 8917 918 – a formation in a child of psychological features, without which it is impossible to master school activity successfully.

Communication 519 317 918 4 – 1. Complex diversified process of establishment and development of contacts among people caused by needs in common activity; it includes the exchange of information, working out of mutual strategy of interaction, perception and understanding of a partner. 2. Realized by symbolic means an interaction of 2 or more subjects, caused by needs in cooperative activity and aimed at important change of a state, behavior and personal sense formation of a partner. It consists in the mental exchange of news with objective and emotional aspects.

Communication: deficit 5189 317 96818 4 – reduction of intensity and quality of communication of a child with other people, usually associated with his being in children institutions of closed type (clinics, children houses, or in families, where parents or educators do not give the child adequate attention). Lack of communication leads to retardation and declination of psychological development.

Nonverbal communication 519 317 918 45 – they are gestures, mime, pantomimicry and other expressive movements.

Communication: structure 619 3107 918 48 – from the viewpoint of social psychology there are such aspects of communication: 1. communicative aspect expressed as the exchange of information, its understanding; in the course of communication an addressee and the sender must use the same symbolic system, they influence on each other. 2 interactive aspect expressed as partners interaction in the organization and performance of common activity; aspect is not only the form of communication, external view of communication, as well kinds of motives and aims of each aspect have their meaning; it was established by researches of such types of interaction as co-friendship, competition and conflict. 3. Perceptual aspect expressed as the acceptance of one partner by the other one.

Communication: leading type 5198 3174 918 4 – a type of communication with people, dominant in the given age period. It influences on the formation of basic personal qualities.

Communication: level 5519 412 918 1 – as to one of approaches there are: 1. macro-level when a man communicates with other people according to the fully formed social relations, traditions and habits 2. Middle level a communication in frames of a theme practiced one time or many times 3. micro-level i.e. an act of a contact, born an element of content and expressed as certain outer marks as simplest elements that are on the base of other levels: answer-question, mime act- etc.

Factorial communication 317 918 4 – out of context communication, used communicative means at the aim of support of the process of communication.

Brotherhood society 518084 31914 – the second primary form of human society e.g. complex of relatives, managed by one of the sons of the previous leader, who governs, supporting on brothers. It is appeared from the 1st form of father horde as the result of murder and eating of a leader by his sons. This event left the indelible traces in history of human evolution in particular conditioned the differentiation of psyche and personality; appearance of new feelings, incest taboo; totemism, religion, morals and social portioning.

Object 5891 42194 81 – a fragment of reality, at which an activity of associated with it subject is aimed. Things, existing independently from the subject, become objects in the course of the subject's interacting with them.

Object: attachment 58191 42194 801 – libidinal ties, distinguished feature of which is the constant fixation of

© Grabovoi G.P., 2003

libido on one certain object or objects.

Object-Libido 42 194 81 319 – libido, turned to an object, associated with sexual objects. Being taken out from objects, again becomes ego-libido.

Object- referential 8911 42194 81 – a person or a group as one of the basic elements of the structure of referential relations, with which a subject of relations consciously or unconsciously corresponding taking and realizing in behavior the models, norms and values of the object or orients on them.

Sexual object 91 642194 89 – the term means a person who suggests a sexual drive or from whom the sexual attraction is originated.

Sexual object: choice 4280794 81 - (a choice of a live object, double choice of the object; - choice of the object in 2 terms) phenomenon of psychosexual development i.e. infantile sexual life, expressed as the double choice of the object, 2 times by 2 pushes. The 1st one begins at the age from 2 to 5 years old and during the period of latent freezing or even regresses; it differs by infantilism of sexual aims. The 2nd one begins in the period of sexual maturity i.e. pubertal period and it's conditioned of the sexual life final forms.

Object sexual: choice: way 58191 42194 89 – there are two main choices of love object, what in their turn are subdivided into some narrow directed ways: 1. narcissistic: a. what you represents by yourself in the image and likeness; b. what you were before; c. what you would like to be; d. a person, who was the part of himself; 2.supporting of: a. feeding woman, b. defending man, c. number of persons succeeded further.

Object sexual: choice: type 0421894 617 – 1. forms of development and orientation of libido, realizing after narcissistic stage: 1.narcissistic type when the more similar to it object takes the place of own ego: 2. the type of support when faces became dear due to satisfaction of other life needs, are chosen as well by libido objects.

Object sexual: narcissistic choice 1984019181 – a

choice of love object in the image and likeness. A try to find oneself, subsequent upon some libido disorders.

Object sexual: 1ˢᵗ choice 80719 418 121 – as to psychoanalysis, it is always unconscious and incestuous; in a man it is directed to mother and a sister; in a woman it does to father and a brother.

Object sexual: finding out: way 1 421 94 81 – a process of finding out of a love object is a secondary meeting (primary one is sucking mothers chest which becomes the pre-image of any love relations), to which 2 way lead: a way based upon pre-images of early childhood, a way narcissistic which is searching the own ego and finds out it in other person. This way is important for pathological exodus.

Objectivation 481519319 41 – a process and result of location of perception images in the outside world where the sources of perceivable information are disposed.

Objectivity 31941 891 168 – 1. Actual existence of things independent of subject's will and consciousness, phenomena and processes, their features and relations of all world in the whole; belonging to the so called objective reality. 2. Content of knowledge, corresponding to a subject. 3. Consistency of objective reality, impartiality, fairness.

Objective 19319041 89 – 1. Existing outside and independent from consciousness, inherent to the object or correspondent to it. 2. Correspondent to reality.

Stunning 521 428 91 – a disorder of consciousness activity by sharp increase of the threshold of perception for all external influences; the perception is difficult, and actions are inhibited at that.

Talent (giftedness) 519 514 31988 – 1. Qualitatively special combination of abilities, providing the success in performance of an activity. Joint action of abilities, which presents certain structure and allows compensating of the lack of separate abilities due to the development of others. 2.Common abilities or general moments of abilities, determining the range of a man's possibilities and level and peculiarity of his activity. 3. Lifeware or intellect, whole

© Grabovoi G.P., 2003

individual characteristic of cognitive abilities and abilities to learn. 4. Complex of properties, natural gifts, type of degree of expression and particularity of abilities natural premises. 5. Talent; presence of interior conditions for outstanding achievements in activity. Multi-meaning of the term denotes the multi-aspects of the problem of the whole approach to the sphere of abilities. Talent as the most general feature of this sphere requires the complex psychological, differential and psychological and social and psychological study.

General giftedness 514 31988 317 – an integral estimation of the level of development of special abilities, associated with the development of concrete abilities, but rather independent from each of them.

Early talent 14 319884 18 – talent special or general, discovered in regard to children. The time of expression of gifts is different in the different areas. It reveals especially early in musical actions, then in drawing. It happens earlier in mathematics corresponding to conceptual areas. It is accompanied by expressed drive to some studies i.e. an inclination to show fancy.

Obsession (possession) 498617 918 1 – a notion of folk and medieval medicine, devoted to explanation of diseases (psychic) reasons; it supposes the evil spirits' possession of physical body of a man. From the viewpoint of science besides religious and ideological premises, the subjective senses of a client could play the role in the genesis of the notion, a disease for him/her is something alien, that deprives him of the power of his/her own body.

Loneliness 591617 88061 – one of psychogenic factors including the emotional state of a man who is under changed (unaccustomed) condition of isolation from other people.

Unambiguity 591614 318 - as to psychodiagnostic methods it means its ability to reflect at a data the feature of phenomenon only, at estimation of which it is aimed. If there are other features as a data, lateral features of a testee not associated with methods i.e. coming out of limits of its validity, then the method is considered not unambiguous though can be practically valid.

Expectation 598 688 716 01 – a notion expressing the ability to foresee the future events. One of the basic notions of cognitive psychology.

Insight 50816121 0981 – sudden, appearing instantly and not originated from previous experience new understanding, comprehension of essential relations, tasks, problems and structure of the whole situation, through which the problem solving is achieved.

Oculography 521 617 918 448 (norm of results) a method of study of eyes motions through the registration of changes of electric potential of retina and eyes muscles.

Oligophrenia 1857422 – a form of mental retardation, characterized by: 1. Property of being total so as all neuropsychic processes are undeveloped. 2. Hierarchy of psychological defects; it is most probably observed the disorders of movement of inner processes in intellectual and speech spheres; less than probably in sensory-motor sphere.

Oligophrenopsychology 1422519 – a part of special psychology studies psychopathic development and possibility of its correction in mental-retarded humans with a heavy form of brain regression. It reveals the reason of their mental retardation (inborn defects of neural system, result of disease or trauma), studies their psychological features, forms and degree of defects display and promotes the creation of programs and methods of their teaching in special schools.

Olfactometer 591 688 71 – a device for the measurement of smell acuteness. Especially spread the Zwaardemaker olfactometer is an empty cylinder with holes, containing a smelling substance, in which a glass tube with a scale input: to the degree of sinking in the cylinder, it decreases the spread of a substance through open hole of the tube to the nose of a testee. Unit of measure of smell acuteness is expressed in centimeters of tube sinking into the cylinder.

Olfactometry 488 71 8194 (standard of measurements

with different instruments) - procedure for measure of the of smell acuity by olfactometer (special instrument). Units of acute sense of smell depend on the type of different used devices.

Id 918411 618 401 – one of personal structure i.e. special psychological instance, unconscious desires and drives. It is localized in the unconscious center of instinctive stimuli , sexual or aggressive striving to immediate satisfaction, independent from subject's relation to outer reality. The most powerful sphere of personality includes denying of the time flow, acting under the principle of pleasure the complex of various unconscious drives, presentations, tendencies, impulses and moving forces of a person.

Ontogenesis 891 618 718 14 – a process of development of an individual organism. In terms of psychology it is the formation of main structures of individual's psyche during his childhood.

Operator 9181017 98 – a man, whose working activity consists in interaction with organs of control of some process on the base of its informational model.

Operator: reliability 19181017 988 (reliability of the human operator) - Psychological qualitative characteristics of a person as an employee, which is provided by the steady performance driven by him the 'man – machine' in the whole range of conditions of its operation.

Operator: hindrance resistance 69181 017 9818 – a psychological feature of readiness of a man to effective performance of actions when hindrances which are characteristically similar to the useful signals are presented. Recognition of useful signals on the background of such hindrances is conjugated with strong nervous tension.

Operator: getting of information 179 98488161 – a system of cognitive operations of an operator, serving for the recognition of signals of outer world.

Operationalization 79881 9 848 12 – a demand which a scientific notion must satisfy. It is used when introducing of a new notion and supposes the precise denotation of concrete procedures, ways, methods or actions through the use of which one may be assured that the given notion is not 'empty' that is the phenomenon denoted that way exists actually.

Operation 118117 97484 — a structural unity of activity correlated with the task and objective conditions of its realization; a way of performance of the activity, defining by conditions of real external or mental situation. The level of operation is filled with skills and automatic actions, and the features of the last are the features of operations. Operations are approximately independent acts, their content responses to not the object of need, but conditions, under which they take place.

Intellectual operation 7897484 489 — a term for the denotation of actions which passed into the internal aspect and become convertible due to the coordination with other mental actions. When actions pass from outer form into inner, they become accessible for reconstruction and conversion.

Concrete operation 117 974814 019 — a notion of operational conception of intellect, means a logical operation, performing on the base of outer, visible data, inherent for children of 7-8 and 11-12 years old. On the base of the performance of concrete operations a child acquires the possibility to foresee results of his/her own acts.

Adaptable operation 7484119 64 1 — belongs to the reactive level of response, the lowest in the hierarchy structure of subject's activity. It appears as the process of involuntary imitation or adaptation to objective conditions of a situation (e.g. adaptation of a child to language conditions).

Conscious operation 7974181401 — is the result of the automation of actions. In the course of repeated recurring of some action (for example, when learning to drive a car or writing), the content of the proper goals at first perceived, takes the place of the execution conditions in the structure of other, more complex actions. Due to the change of the place of purpose in the structure of activities and target shift on the condition arising when the automation of action carrying out, this action turns into a conscious operation.

Formal operation 918 1149481 9 – a stage of intellectual development. It is typical for children from 11 to12 and from 14 to15 years old. It is to be a system of operations of the second order, 'overbuilt' over concrete operation. Acquired the formal operations, a child can build own, hypothetic deductive reasoning, based on independent hypothesis and real control of their effects. When reasoning of the kind, it appears the possibility to change for symbols of universal nature the concrete relations.

Recognition (identification) 489712 61841 – a process of classifying of a perceivable object as one of some previously fixed classes, because of what the construction of conscious perceptive image takes place. The important moment of these processes is the result of comparison of perceptive description of an object with preserved in memory models of the description of relevant classes.

Simultaneous recognition 182 61841 418 – ranging of a perceivable object in some class as the result of instant spontaneous decision.

Successive recognition 7812 618419819 – ranging of a perceivable object in a class as the result of detailed step-by-step and consequent analysis of its features.

Mediation 428614 318 41089 – relation of one notion (object) to other mental or recognizable only through the third, so, that a mediate notion acts as the base for correlation of original notions (objects). It characterizes the structure of a process or an activity in an aspect of achievement of aims and results. Objective embodiment of the structure of mediation is the mean.

Mediation through action 14 8160 49164101 – methodological principle, reflecting the determination of mental processes in an individual consciousness, also interpersonal processes in groups. It is considered as the system organizing feature of a collective, defining its important social and psychological characteristics.

Sign mediation 141319 41089 – a basic notion means the way of behavior control, realizing by an individual. In this theory all psychic development is considered as the change of the structure of psychic processes due to conclusion in it of a sign (symbol), what leads to the transformation of natural immediate processes into cultural, mediate.

Dementalising 890418 9819 741 – a philosophic notion, means the process, where human abilities pass in to an object and become embodied in it, because of what the object becomes a social-cultural. As to activity, it is dementalized not only as outer result, but because of qualities of the activity subject; changing the world, a person changes himself or herself.

Questioning 98019 614 9817 – a method of psychological study, when people are asked questions, on the base of answers the conclusion of their psyche is made.

Questionnaire 614 88 91 9817 – a method of social and psychological research through tests. In social sciences it is performed to clear up biography data, opinion, value orientation, social attitudes and personal features.

Questionnaire close 198 614 98171 – methodology matter of which supposes the questions to which the client has to answer or statements with which he/she has to agree or disagree.

Questionnaire (checklist) 419 9817 3194 – proposes a possibility to get information about a client, not directly reflecting his personal features. It may be biography questionnaire or questionnaires of interests or purposes depending on how much properly finding out particular interests or purposes bear a relationship to personal features.

Questionnaire closed 1019 6184 98917 (questionnaire of closed type) - suggests a selection of questions' answers from the options offered in the questionnaire.

Questionnaire of creativity 9 6184 98167 – a mean of the diagnostics of creative abilities of an individual. It is the list of situations, senses, interests, forms of behavior, typical for creative persons. It may be addressed either to a testee or to his environment.

Personality questionnaire 198 4614 98178 – class of psychodiagnostic methods, devoted to the definition of a degree of expression of certain personal features. It is complex of methodological means for the study and evaluation of separate features and of displays of personality. Each methodology is standardized list consisted of a set of sentences, the content of which a testee may agree with or disagree.

Minnesota Multiphase Personality Enquirer (MMPI) 19 614 98917 18 – the method of psychodiagnostic research of individual features and psychic states of personality. In the course of a research 550 statements are proposed to a testee, modeling his attitude to various life situations, and he must chose one of three answers: 'right', 'wrong', 'cannot say'. Significant answers are fixed with the help of special 'keys', after quantitative processing are written down in the sheet, which has 3 estimating and 10 basic scales.

Open questionnaire 981019 6184 98917 (questionnaire of open type) – supposes free form of the suggested questions answering.

Typological questionnaire 48 98917 918 – it is to be worked out on the base of the definition of a personality types which allows to bring a testee to one or other type, different in qualitatively specific manifestations.

Personal features questionnaire 198 6814 91817 – measure the expression of features i.e. constant personal characteristics.

Optimism 498 9171 81948 – as the feature of a personality it reflects proportional development of all psychic processes, provides a cheerful world view, belief in people, their power and abilities, assurance of social progress and belief in own forces as a subject of activity.

Experience 489107191 – 1. Complex of practically acquired skills, knowledge. 2. Received as the result of active practical interaction with the world the reflection on consciousness of the world laws and social practice. 3. The same as experiment: reproduction of phenomena, creation of something new under certain conditions at the aim of a trial or study. 4. Attempt to do something.

Dual blind experience 107191 218 – a special experimental procedure, when not only a testee knows about senses and features of the experiment, but also an experimenter does. So, the possibility of experimenter's influence on the results of the experiment are excluded, and the marks of its objectivity increases. Such conditions may be modeling by a computer.

Organ 814 317 914 817 – 1. Animal or vegetative organism's part, having certain structure and function. 2. Mean, instrument of something.

Sensory organ 214 712 514 312 – nervous receptors, serving as the receivers of signals, informing of changes in outer world (exteroception) and in a subject's organism.

Organization 918471 318 9421 – in psychological aspect a differential and mutual disciplines unity of individuals and groups, acting on the base of joint aims, interests and programs.

Organization: conflict: type 7191 318 94821 (conflict types at organization) – the reasoning of typology as follows: 1) aims of a conflict participants; 2) correlation of their actions to existing norms 3) final results of a conflict interaction 4) influence of a conflict on the development of an organization.

Informal organization 4781 3118 9421 – is the unity of people, associated by personal choice and immediate informal contacts. It may appear either in the frames of a formal organization at the aim of either satisfaction of its members' demands which are beyond the limits or independently from it i.e. on the base of non-professional and extraoccupational interests.

Pre-genital organization 14 3198 9421 17 – such organization of sexual life, for which genital zones don't have dominant meaning.

Formal organization 71 318 9429 – it has administrative juridical status and subordinates an individual relative to faceless functional ties and standards of behavior. In the context social-psychological phenomena are organized, conditioned upon such relations as person occupation; collective subdivision, leadership of government and etc.

Organism 419 312 819 212 – 1. living organism i.e. living body, living creature (plants, animals, a man). 2. Complex of spiritual and physical features of a man 3. Complex organized unity.

Organism: orientation 12 819 21298 - subjective localization in the system space and time are produced according to certain criteria (thermal, optical, acoustic, electrical type) with innate mechanisms. Innate components of orientation play a special role for the animals' migrations which use terrestrial or celestial landmarks and sometimes the magnetic field of the Earth.

Orgone 519417 819 14 – universal cosmic living energy i.e. psychic-sexual energetic base of human life.

Horde 981 716319 14 – 1. Old name of the primary form of social organization; primitive horde 2. Disordered, unorganized crowd of people.

Horde fatherly 319 14 819 417 – primary form of a society that is complex of relations under the unlimited rule of a strong male. As a result of murder and eating of 'chief' by his sons transfer into second fraternity society has taken place.

Finding one's bearing 388617 819 14 (orientation) – 1. Definition of a place in space; start with relative to the sides of Earth especially the East. 2. Ability to clear up a situation. Awareness of something. 3. Direction of some activity.

Orientation: type 56917 8139 14 (principle)– (two types of orientation, two principles of orientation) main variants of people orientation towards definition of the position characterized by the difference between 'herd' and 'human' nature; 1) orientation to a herd expresses the human essence as a herd animal, whose actions are determined by instinctive impulses of following a leader, contacts with a herd, loyalty to it. 2) orientation to intellect expresses a man essence as a thinking creature, having consciousness, self-consciousness, individuality and certain independence.

Heterosexual orientation 5117 819 1469 – a drive to subjects of opposite gender.

Homosexual orientation 816 14 21 148 – a drive to subjects of the same gender.

Professional orientation 17 819 148 419 – a system of measure of involving of a person in the world of work; complex of psycho-pedagogical and medicine measures, aimed at optimization of work, work of young people in regard with their desires, abilities and with the control of needs of national production and a society.

Psychoanalytic orientation 78 894119 148 - concept which means a focus of social and philosophical, psychological, and other ideas and concepts: Freud, his disciples and followers, reformers and modernizers of psychoanalysis, as well as various philosophers, sociologists, psychologists, clinicians, and others, in whose work the idea psychoanalysis play a significant role .

Psycho-sexual orientation 617 819 148 – a direction of a sexual drive, process of its development and forms of realization. Its formation includes the pubertal period of sexuality (from 12 to 18 years) and transition sexual period (from 16 to 26 years). Its establishment is the final stage of psycho-sexual development, where the formation of platonic, erotic and sexual libido occurs, and their correspondent main display: erotic fancy, games, sexual fancy, masturbation start of sexual life, incidents and regular sexual life.

Value orientation 781 9 148 191 - the concept of social psychology used in two senses: 1) the ideological, political, moral, aesthetic and other reasons' estimates of subject of reality and orientation in it, and 2) the method of differentiation of individual objects according to their importance. Value orientations are formed in the assimilation of social experience and are found in order, ideals, beliefs, interests, and other manifestations of personality. They are closely related to its cognitive and volitional sides in the structure of the activities. The system forms the content side of their personality orientation and expresses the inner basis of its relationship to reality.

Orientation: type 214 716 319 14 - different strategies of survey of the surroundings determine the effectiveness and quality of the assimilated knowledge and skills of the subject: 1) the orientation of the first type is based on occasional symptoms, so the training is conducted by trial and error and gives poor results, 2) the orientation of the second type is based on attributes and relationships gleaned empirically adequate only for the assignment, here education is closer to an adequate, but the results do not have the capability to transfer skills and knowledge generated by new relationships, and 3) the orientation of the third type is based on material properties and relations, dedicated by analyzing the internal structure of the object, and therefore acquire knowledge and skills can be transferred to new, changed conditions.

Instrument 596 317 819 148 – 1. Technical device, with help of which a work or action is performed. 2. Mean for achievement of an aim.

Psychological instrument 528 912 614 18 – an element of the psychic function structure, role of which is similar to a tool in a man labor activity structure.

Comprehension 298678 919 148 – a feature of perception which existed at the level of consciousness and characterized by the personal level of perception i.e. a feature to prescribe to perceivable object or phenomenon a certain sense to denote it by words and to relate it to certain language category.

Base (foundation) 592 541 619 18 – 1. Source, principal, on what something is built, a thing which is the essence of something. 2. Original, main concepts of something.

Age feature 319 1418 914 17 – in terms of psychology specific features of a personality, of an individual, his psyche, regularly changing during the change of age phases of development. Their characteristic is based on the reveal of psychological content of the process of development of cognitive abilities and personality formation at successive age stages of ontogenesis. Age features form certain complex of various traces, including cognitive, motivational, emotional, and perceptual etc.

Day residue 528 614319 12 – followed from day impressions, which became the reason of dream formation.

Active touch 918491 – a way of the image organization of an object through its intentional touching. The kinesthetic senses plays a leading role here.

Instrumental touch 528 617 31918 – a process of formation of a touch image of an object through additional tools, when tactile signals pass to a hand from a touching object through this tool.

Passive touch 91 617 318918 – a process of formation of a touch image of an object as the result of its removal relatively the immovable hand or fingers.

Selection 508 614 319 18 – extraction of somebody, something from environment, a number or amount on the base of some criteria, features.

Natural selection 5108 6814 319 18 –a conception, according to which species, less adapted for a survive under the given conditions, die or are eliminated giving place for more adaptable which give their features to their posterity.

Professional selection 15089 319 18 – a variant of psychological selection i.e. an making of a stuff decisions on the base of study and prognostic values of suitability of people to master a profession, to perform duties and to achieve the level of master. It is the system of means, providing prognostic values of inter-correspondence of a man and a profession towards types of activity, which performed under the normative given dangerous conditions (hygienic, climatic, technical, social), and which claimed high responsibility, health, workability, precision in performance of tasks and stability of emotional-volitional regulation.

Psychological selection 508 614 418 189 – an acceptance of the solving of suitable candidates for learning or professional activity with account of the results of psychological and psychophysiologic trials. It is used when managing of an industry, aviation, army, sport and etc.

Responsibility 517 314 81911 – taking various forms of the control of a subject's activity from a perspective of accepted norms and rules performance by him.

Refusal (denial, rejection) 31918 617 19 – a fact (indicator) witnessed that some desire cannot be satisfied.

Forced refusal 16178 19648161 – an act and emotional stress of denial from satisfaction of drives, caused by unfavorable inter psychic or external circumstances, or their combination.

Involuntary real denial 6178 191 519413 collective term that means different adverse conditions and factors contributing to the emergence of the disease. These may include: a lack of love in life, material disadvantage, family discord, unhappy marriage, unfavorable social conditions and strict moral requirements for the personality.

Attitude (position, relation) 528 147 818 14181 – a subjective side of the reflection of reality, the result of interaction of a man with the world. In terms of psychology it is inter-disposition of objects and their features. It may be presented among changing objects, phenomena or features, and in case of a separated constant object in its ties with other objects, phenomena, features.

Maternal attitude 71 8189 141871 – a type of associated and psychotherapeutic procedure, aimed at establishment of relations between a doctor and a client, similar to the relation of mother and a child.

Intergroup relation 47 818 1841319 – in terms of psychology the complex of social-psychological phenomena, characterizing subjective reflection, perception of various ties, appearing among social groups as well as caused by them group interactions' approach.

Interpersonal relation 1847 8198 7181 (personalized) – subjectively experienced relationships among people, objectively displayed in a character and a way of mutual influences of people in common activity and communication. The system of attitudes, orientation, expectation and other dispositions, through which people perceive and evaluate each other. These dispositions are mediated by contents, aims, values and organization of common activity and act as the base of formation of social-psychological climate in team.

Inter-ethnic relation 528 147 818 4849 – subjectively experienced relations among people of different nations. It is expressed as attitudes and orientations to inter-ethnic contacts in various spheres of interaction, national stereotypes, moods and behavior, acts of people and concrete ethnic communities.

Attitude subject reflexive 55298 318712 - reflexive relations internalized system of the subject with other people, based on the mind's ability to reflect the position of the 'other' or ideas about the features of their own vision of the object of the problem. These relationships are the necessary component of the cognitive activity of the subject, for the reconstruction of the outlooks of others on the subject matter can be seen in its new dimensions and stimulates critical thinking which allows making reflection to be an internal dialogue with other significant people.

Reflection 519614319 1 – the universal feature of matter, consists in the ability of objects to reproduce features, structural characteristics and relations of other objects.

Psychic reflection 9614431981 2 – in the transition from biological form to the psychic there are such stages: 1. sensory characterized by reflection of separate irritants: response to only biological important irritants; 2. perceptual a transition to which is expressed as the ability to reflect the complex of irritants; it starts the orientation in the complex of features, responded to neutral biological irritants; 3. intellectual displays so as in addition to reflection of a separate objects the reflection of their functional relations and ties arises.

Responsiveness 819 417 319 14 – a process of display of an experience sidewise, accompanied by sharp colored emotion and emotional release, associated with traumatic event.

Denial of reality 419 716 91891 – a defensive mechanism, rejecting the existence of outer dangerous factors.

Retardation 498792 618 19 – disposition or place at lower level of development than others.

Mental retardation 792 6181 19 – a disorder of general development psychic and intellectual, caused by lack of the central nervous system. It has tough, ignorant character.

Driving back 891 618 017 21 – a process of reduction of criticism and formation of a compromise. Sometimes it is considered as the process of transformation of artifacts, occurring in an individual's development. It is the main scheme of dream appearance and of all psychopathic presentations.

Speech report 218617 31918 (subjective report, subjective data, phenomenal data, self-observation data) – a report of a testee when naïve (non-introspective, non-analytic) positioning.

Alienation (estrangement) 41811873 198 – a process and result of transformation of features, abilities and people activity into something another than it is e.g. the transformation into independent force, dominant over people. In terms of psychology a display of such life relation of a subject and the world, when the products of his activity, he himself, and other persons or groups, being the bearers of certain norms, precepts and values, are considered as opposite to him from non-similarity to rejection and hostility. It is expressed as correspondent senses of a subject:

sense of isolation, loneliness, rejection, loss of ego etc.

Error (mistake) 987 611 3054 – inaccuracy, wrongness in actions and thoughts.

Operator error 118 611 3054 – increase of established limits means the damage of normal function of ergatic system. For the characteristics of a situation where an error achieves meanings which make impossible of aims achievement, for which the ergatic system was made, there is used the notion 'operator denial'.

Error of stimulus 498712 3054 – a response to introspective experiences, expressed in the terms of extrinsic senses, but not in the terms of own senses and their qualities. It is a known term in introspective psychology, reflecting its atomistic direction.

Sensation (feeling) 519671 319 14 – construction of images of separate features of objects of outer world in the process of immediate interaction with it.

Sensation: interaction 3198 14 814 – their regularities show how the thresholds of perception are changed under simultaneous influence of several stimuli.

Sensation: duration 71 319 14 89148 – a feature of perception, consists in the fact that time interval in the course of which the sense takes place, doesn't correlate with duration of an irritant influence as a rule. The sense appears some time after the influence beginning, and may disappear only in some time after the influencing finish.

Sense: intensity 8914 31 71 369 141 – a degree of subjective expression of a sense, associated with an irritant.

Sense: classification 671 319 1412 – division of senses towards the criterion of their relation with analyzers, responsible for their appearance. So, there are highlighted visual, acoustic, tactile, olfactive, gustable, proprioreceptive, motorial and etc.

Pain sense 1 3194 14 819 – senses, typical for such influences, that may lead to the damage of the wholeness of an organism.

Kinesthetic sense 19 14519 614 – a sense, giving a

subject the information of movement and position of his body. It is shown as the irritation of proprioreceptors, placed in muscles, joints, ligaments and chords.

Organic sense 319 671 391 14 – senses, indicating of the certain current processes of an organism associated with organic needs. It may have local character and stimulate for filling in of a concrete substance, which is in need for the organism. They are senses of hungry, thirst, pain etc. and associated with sexual activity.

Tactile sense 1319 148 1619 – a form of skin sensitivity, characterized by the work of two types of receptors: 1) nervous plexus, surrounding hair bulbs; 2) receptors, consisting of cells of the attached tissue of capsules. Senses, arising by a touch, pressure, vibration etc. have various character.

Temperature sense 9 14 5819 61419 – a type of skin senses, revealed in the senses of warmth and cold.